Lebrecht, Norman

Music in London

Hertfordshire
COUNTY COUNCIL

Please return this book
on or before the last
date shown or ask for

Please renew or return items by the date
shown on your receipt

www.hertsdirect.org/libraries

Renewals and enquiries: 0300 123 4049

Textphone for hearing or 0300 123 4041
speech impaired users:

Hertfordshire

L32

22 JUN 2006

L33

MUSIC
IN
LONDON

NORMAN LEBRECHT

AURUM PRESS

To my friends in the London orchestras

First published in Great Britain 1992
by Aurum Press Ltd,
10 Museum Street, London WC1A 1JS
Copyright © 1989, 1992 by Norman Lebrecht

Originally published in France 1991 by
Éditions Bernard Coutaz

A catalogue record for this book is available
from the British Library

ISBN 1 85410 223 0

1   3   5   7   9   10   8   6   4   2
1993   1995   1996   1994   1992

Typeset by Tradespools Ltd., Frome, Somerset
Printed in Great Britain by Butler and
Tanner Ltd, Frome

CONTENTS

ACKNOWLEDGEMENTS

This book was conceived as part of a French series edited by the late Maurice Fleuret and produced by Bernard Coutaz and Isa Guyoux, all of whom were generous in their support and enthusiasm. Elbie Lebrecht laboured day and night over the picture research (picture credits are on p.177). For all sorts of other ideas and services connected with this book I am indebted (alphabetically) to: John Amis, the late Hermann Baron, Fred Barschak, Andrew Burn, Anthony Camden, Alexander Chancellor, Michael Church, John Denison, Anne Freeman, Rodney Friend, Josef and Irene Fröhlich, Clive and Penny Gillinson, Berthold Goldschmidt, Victor Hochhauser, Lennox Mackenzie, David Mellor, Terry Morton, Eleanor Rosé, Daniel Snowman, Lucy Tuck, Joeske van Walsum, Christel Wallbaum, John Willan.

PREFACE

The history of music in London has yet to be written, and this book does not attempt to do more than sketch its outline. The full story is an extraordinary one – of a city that dominated the musical world without producing a major composer of its own; of a people's triumph over philistine rulers; of an open mind and purse readily extended to creative spirits.

Music in London is a subject unto itself, separate from its development in the rest of the kingdom. For while the best and worst of British art was always to be found in the capital, it often defied national trends and tastes. A cosmopolitan metropolis, London gazed initially eastwards to Rome, then northwards to Scandinavia until, in 1066, its commercial and cultural interests were permanently tied across the Channel to France and central Europe. London is regularly accused, not without cause, of turning its back on the rest of the country and imbibing indiscriminately from the Continent. London, sniffed Joseph Chamberlain, mayor of Birmingham, 'is the clearing-house of the world.'[1]

In musical terms, the absence of intellectual import controls was a mixed blessing. Some indigenous creators were severely inhibited by the influx of greater minds, others were inspired by their ideas. The result was a musical environment of remarkable diversity. 'When a man is tired of London he is tired of life,' declared the dictionarist Samuel Johnson, 'for there is in London all that life can afford.'[2] Johnson was tone-deaf, but his aphorism aptly expresses the city's musical variety.

In this brief account of the city's essential musical character and dynamics, many notable individuals and fascinating incidents of the past millennium have been omitted. Seekers of Gilbert

Hogarth's eighteenth-century view of music in London.

and Sullivan anecdotes, Grieg's residences or Gregorian chant will need to consult other titles recommended in the reading list. The purpose of this volume is to examine the social, political and technological factors that have raised London to its self-proclaimed status as 'music capital of the world'.

Norman Lebrecht
St John's Wood
April 1992

PART ONE

1

━━━━━

THE TONELESS TOWN

Musical London – the combination is an unnatural one, almost a contradiction in terms. Music and London are historically mismatched, an odd couple, neither having contributed appreciably to the advancement of the other. Music drew its strength from the chapels of France and Italy and the folk-wit of central Europe. London grew mighty on commerce, imperial conquest and a language unconstrained by despotism. Where music is a triumph of the spirit, London is a monument to materialism. Music is structured and sensual, London amorphous and impersonal – 'a horribly unmusical city,'[1] in the words of its sharpest critic.

What else could be expected of the heart and capital of the notorious 'land without music'? England, so abundant in literary and intellectual talent, seemed to lack the instinctive gift of melody. For centuries it produced no significant composer. Prolific and profitable in every other sector, it showed a desperate trade deficit in structured harmony. Like present-day Japan it imported European music and yielded little in response except heavy applause and hard cash.

'England,' declared the American poet-philosopher Ralph Waldo Emerson with customary finality, 'has no music.'[2] Friedrich Nietzsche diagnosed a musical 'defect'[3] in the English soul, which lacked rhythm and movement. Heinrich Heine found a people with 'no ear, either for rhythm or music, and whose unnatural passion for playing the piano and singing is therefore all the more repulsive'.[4] If an immortal poet, a philosopher and a poet-philosopher separately confirmed the symptoms, the country's melodic condition must have been positively moribund.

Yet, at the very moment of Heine's visit in 1827, London enjoyed

1

a richer concert diet than Berlin; was sustaining the dying Beethoven while Vienna raved over Rossini; was feeding great composers with operatic storylines; and was enticing legendary songbirds to its busy stages. Though it lacked a native-born musical genius, the city throbbed with musical life. Liszt and Mendelssohn were recent débutants; Weber had written an opera for Covent Garden and had died nearby. 'Home, Sweet Home', a ditty from an indigenous opera, was stolen by Donizetti and sung around the world (Richard Strauss would later repeat the plagiarism). Late Beethoven quartets, shunned for their perplexity in Paris and Berlin, were played at amateur soirées organized by a manager of *The Times*.

What prompted George Bernard Shaw decades later to indict this 'horribly unmusical city' was not its indifference to music but 'our Gargantuan musical digestion',[5] an indiscriminate appetite for sounds of all shapes, colours and sizes. London, said the philosopher Thomas Hobbes in earlier times, 'has a great belly but no palate'.[6] This reckless gourmandise persists in its present-day eminence.

Since the Second World War, London has proclaimed itself music capital of the world. It sustains more international orchestras and opera companies than any other metropolis, greater variety than Vienna, more maestri than Milan, an audience younger than New York's and more passionate than the Parisian. It is the epicentre of the record industry, trend-setter of the pop scene, home of major music publishers and source of indispensable scholarship. Could such fecundity ever have arisen in a fundamentally music-less spot?

Das Land ohne Musik is a hoary old libel that requires rapid demolition. Although England's compositional sterility was long the target of cheap continental jokes, it was 1914 before the abusive cliché appeared in print, as the title of a set of socio-political essays by a respected German commentator, Oscar A. H. Schmitz.[7] A biographer of Disraeli and admirer of the English way of life, Schmitz tuned into rising bilateral hostility to focus his tract on the enemy's Achilles' heel. 'The English,' he alleged, 'are the only cultured race without a music of their own (popular melodies excepted).'[8] To German readers, this confirmed their innate superiority over an adversary unkissed by the muse and Schmitz enumerated further physical and spiritual deficiencies in the English: 'Not only are their ears less discerning [than ours], but their whole inner life must be poorer ... Music lends wings and

Frontispiece of Schmitz's inflammatory tract.

makes everything appear wonderful and intelligible ... Through music we understand nature and the souls of men. Our pains and disappointments are resolved in music and love is intensified. Our emotions flow and our joy sings out.'[9] The English, on the other hand, were heartless boors.

The book sold barely 8,000 copies in Germany, but its title became a catchphrase among musicians the world over. By the time *The Land without Music* gained wider currency in an English edition in 1925,[10] Schmitz had anyway changed his tune.

After the war, he turned his attention homeward on *Das rätselhafte Deutschland (Mysterious Germany)*, attacking his compatriots as 'a nation of sergeants and travelling salesmen'[11] and calling for a united Europe under the leadership of England – a land that was

3

allegedly without music or human emotion.

Musically, Germany had lost more in the war than the cream of its youth. It had been forced to surrender two centuries of musical hegemony. The three Bs – Bach, Beethoven, Brahms – were waning, for want of reinforcement. Neither Bruckner nor Reger made an impact abroad; Strauss and Mahler were subverters of tradition; and Arnold Schoenberg's patriotic mission to 'ensure the supremacy of German music for the next 100 years'[12] with his twelve-note method of composition was too arcane to be widely practised. Nor was it long before Schoenberg was banished and his works banned throughout the Reich. The tonal wellsprings had dried up in Germany, and no dominant alternative presented itself elsewhere.

The revolutionary spark that glimmered so promisingly in Russian music was snuffed out by Stalin's repressions. American composers were in isolationist prairie mood, the French composers were following Satie-esque idiosyncrasies and jazzy hedonism, and Italian opera fell silent with the death of Puccini. Dominance in music shifted, gradually and by default, to the unlikeliest of locations.

London's emergence at the hub of musical life came about neither overnight nor in a rush of creativity. It was not, as some wishfully pretend, the outcome of a glorious English Musical Renaissance, for only the most blinkered Little Englander would imagine that the personalities of Elgar and Delius, Vaughan Williams and Holst, were compelling enough to turn their capital into the *umbilicus mundi*. This modest flowering of composers, arriving after two centuries of stagnant imitation, recovered a modicum of national respectability by making isolated contributions to the world's concert repertoire – Elgar with Enigma Variations and the cello concerto, Vaughan Williams with Greensleeves and the Tallis Fantasia, Holst resoundingly with The Planets and Delius with impressionistic aquarelles and encores. The Union Jack fluttered once again on the fringes of the concert platform, but a generation would pass before its presence was confirmed by a talent of global magnitude.

If London has three Bs, then Benjamin Britten was the only composer among them. The other two were enterprising conductors – Thomas Beecham, who founded a spate of orchestras and opera companies regardless of financial risk and social consequences, and Adrian Boult, architect of music broadcasting and curator of a central performing tradition. But the efforts of individual musicians were never enough to turn the toneless town into a musical Mecca. The making of musical London rests mainly on factors beyond cultural comprehension, amid the tangled thickets of twentieth-century politics and technology. London was elevated not by three immortal Bs but by three mundane Hs: Hitler, Hi-fi and Henry J. Wood.

Its ascent can be dated precisely. At 8 p.m. Greenwich Mean Time on Saturday, 10 August 1895, the state of music in British society was irrevocably altered by a conductor of twenty-six years of age. Raising the baton in a hall built in Queen Victoria's honour at the shopless top of Regent Street, Henry Joseph Wood opened a 10-week season of nightly Promenade Concerts with a bill of twenty-two musical items, none of them weightier than Wagner's immature *Rienzi* overture. Seats were ripped out of the centre of Queen's Hall and standing tickets were sold at an affordable shilling apiece. An ornamental fountain was installed in the middle of the promenade floor. Ices, flowers and cigars were vended from franchised stalls around its perimeter. SMOKING PERMITTED announced the concert hoardings. REFRAIN FROM STRIKING MATCHES contradicted a prominent sign behind the orchestra.

People from all walks of life would drop in casually before or after dinner to a Henry Wood Prom. Master and butler, customer and shop-girl, cabinet minister and cab-driver shared the musical

Proms milieu, 1922.

experience in Queen's Hall, albeit at different price levels. The upper-class grip on musical life was loosened, then broken, by the pioneering Proms.

The concept was not in itself innovatory. Three flamboyant Frenchmen, Philippe Musard, Louis Antoine Jullien and Jules Rivière, had previously dished up summer concerts in which the audience was encouraged to walk about (*se promener*) and take the evening air. Wood's inaugural concerts resembled the frothy lightness of his predecessors', and for much of his vocational life he continued to sweeten his menus with syrupy ballads and piquant piano numbers. His subversive intentions were revealed at the first Wednesday Prom, when a superb account of Schubert's Unfinished (and still unfamiliar) Symphony was squeezed in between the sweetmeats. It was followed days later by the Prelude to Richard Strauss's brand-new opera, *Guntram*. Wood meant to build an audience for serious music by insidious means, gradually thickening the substance of his musical offerings in the most relaxed of ambiences.

By the dawn of the century he had conducted the first performance in London of more than one hundred pieces of music. He gave symphonies by Mahler and Sibelius before Vienna or Berlin heard them, brought over Schoenberg and Skryabin when they were anathema everywhere else, and told his players when they grumbled over abstruse modernisms, 'Stick to it, gentlemen! Stick to it! This is nothing to what you'll have to play in twenty-five years' time!'[13] In half a century of Proms, he introduced some 900 new works to London, of which 285 were world premières. Most of the novelties were by Englishmen, but there were also two landmarks in music history – the first performance anywhere of Schoenberg's atonal 'Five Orchestral Pieces' and the first all-Bartók orchestral concert. 'It is probably difficult for us,' eulogized the belletrist Sacheverell Sitwell, 'to have any conception of how rare was good music before Sir Henry Wood made it the business of his life to bring it nightly before the public. How many ... have gone to the Proms for the first time because there was nothing else to do and then attended, night after night, as often as it was possible!'[14]

Yet, despite their immense appeal, the Proms continually lost money. An initial deficit of £2,000, and several subsequent debts, were covered by a Harley Street laryngologist, Dr George C. Cathcart, whose patients included many well-known singers. Two conditions were attached to his subsidy: that his young friend Wood must conduct every single performance, and that the concert pitch

I remember three performances when Sir Henry Wood conducted my works. The first took place immediately after the 1st world war, probably in Aug. 1920: he introduced my 1st orchestral suite in a prom. concert to the London public; I got news about the performance from the late Philip Heseltine (Peter Warlock), the fervent pioneer of contemporary music. During the war, my works were not allowed to be performed in England, because of my being call "enemy" alien, therefore this first performance after a long period of silence had a certain significance importance.

Later, perhaps about 1930, there was a performance in a B.B.C. studio — a kind of a hanger on the left bank of the Thames (the new building near Queens Hall was not yet finished at that time) — with my Rhapsody, Op 1 for piano and orchestra, with me as soloist), again the 1st Suite, and my "Mandarin" music. Sir Henry kindly invited me to his house before the rehearsals, in order to talk over the tempi etc. of the works. — This was a "landmark" in my career: it was the first orchestra concert devoted entirely to my works.

And finally, in Jan. 1936 there was a B.B.C. concert at Queens Hall with Sir Henry as conductor, and with an All-Hungarian program: works by Liszt, Kodály, and my 2nd piano concerto, again with me as soloist.

I remember these occasions with deep gratitude towards Sir Henry Wood, for his love and care for these novelties, and for his great achievement in recreating them.

Béla Bartók

Bartók was one of many composers to acknowledge a debt to Henry Wood.

should be lowered by a semitone, making life a little easier for the strained throats exposed in his consulting-rooms.

Since Handel's time, when tuning forks gave 422.5 vibrations on the note A, local concert pitch had crept up inexorably by a whole tone to A = 452.5. Cathcart's welcome intervention brought London back into line with the rest of Europe at the French-set *diapason normal* of A = 435. (In modern times it has crept up to 440, still below some European capitals, where hazardous highs above 450 are commonly heard.)

Cathcart was succeeded as benefactor by a German-born banker, Edward Speyer, as the Proms ran into further financial trouble and finally into full-blown crisis when Robert Newman, the Queen's Hall manager, died in 1926. The series was rescued by the British Broadcasting Corporation, newly charged by Parliament with responsibilities for public enlightenment and anxious to play an active musical role. Wood was retained as conductor, but was ordered to renounce his low-brow ballads. His cult of informality survives, nevertheless, to this very day.

Wander past the Royal Albert Hall on any late summer's morning and you will see a queue of sneakered youngsters snaking around the rotunda, awaiting cheap tickets, exchanging musical chit-chat, studying for exams, making intimate assignations. The standing throng at night greets conductors with a ribald barracking and, if the performance pleases, an explosive ovation. The Last Night of the Proms winds down into mindless nostalgia with a Fantasia on British Sea-Songs set by Henry Wood himself and the communal yelling of the jingoist hymn, 'Rule, Britannia!' Despite insolvency, two world wars and the destruction of their home, the Proms survive indestructibly.

Wood's achievement, however, amounted to more than the invention of a summer tradition and the extension of audiences. In the course of his herculean task, he created the first of London's great orchestras and violently caused the birth of the second. Every day for ten weeks, morning and night, he would steer his players through programmes of unimaginable length and unprecedented complexity, with just one rehearsal and with a technique that became famous for its clarity. 'Don't worry,' one nervous player was assured by his neighbour, 'you may be sight-reading this piece tonight, but you can't possibly go wrong with *that* stick in front of you!'[15]

No orchestra in the world was ever so rigorously trained. At 9.45 each morning, fifteen minutes ahead of schedule, Wood would enter the rehearsal room, greet every player by name with 'Good Morning, Mr X!' and a tap of his tuning fork, and wait beside each instrument until it was perfectly tuned. At 9.58 he mounted the rostrum. On the last chime of ten from All Souls' steeple in Langham Place he swept down the baton. Only once did he arrive late, blaming a delayed train, and he turned down many a more comfortable occupation – including the conductorship of the Boston Symphony Orchestra in 1920 – in order to persist with his Proms.

His immaculate self-discipline infected the most indifferent of players. Strauss called the Queen's Hall Orchestra 'a little colony of artists'[16] and Debussy was dumbfounded when they played spontaneously to the end of a perfect *Fêtes* after he, an inept conductor, had lost his beat and laid down the baton. 'I fancy he went back to Paris with something to think about,'[17] crowed Wood. Schoenberg, never generous with his praise, was 'extraordinarily pleased with the orchestra'.[18]

Wood was determined to eradicate the corruptions that pervaded orchestral life, and in 1904 he abolished the privilege that allowed players to send unrehearsed deputies to a concert if they found a better-paid job for themselves. He offered personal

Sir Henry Wood, known to his men as 'Timber'.

contracts for a minimum of 150 concerts a year, in return for promised attendance at all sessions unless certified sick.

The players duly signed, ignoring the restrictive clause, and
when Wood turned up one morning to find a band of strange
faces, he stormed off, leaving Newman to announce categorically
'Gentlemen, in future there will be no deputies!'[19] Forty-six of the
players, about half the orchestra, interpreted this as an infringe-
ment of their time-honoured liberties and immediately resigned.
Wood replaced them with students and continued his season.

Three renegade hornists and a trumpeter, travelling together by
train, resolved that the rebels would form their own band, the London Symphony Orchestra. They hired the venerable Hans Richter
as conductor, booked Queen's Hall one summer's afternoon (most
played again that night at Covent Garden) and plastered the bill-
boards with deprecatory comments about their former employer.
Wood, to his everlasting credit, conspicuously attended the concert and applauded their début.

The LSO modelled its autonomy on the Berlin Philharmonic and
formed close ties with its legendary conductor, the 'magician',
Arthur Nikisch. In 1912 it toured the USA, the first British orches-

Arthur Nikisch, 'The Magician'.

10

tra to venture abroad, and on its return preserved a fragment for posterity, taking Nikisch to the offices of the Gramophone Company at Hayes, to make acetate recordings of Beethoven's *Egmont* overture and one of Liszt's Hungarian Rhapsodies. The foundations for London's modern musical industry had been well and truly laid.

Around this time, a wealthy young conductor was looking around for an orchestra he could call his own. Thomas Beecham, son of a Lancashire laxative manufacturer, was Wood's age, twenty-six, when he gave his first London concert. He engaged half the Queen's Hall band at a small hall on Wigmore Street, and flopped miserably.

After further forays with a New Symphony Orchestra and a Beecham Symphony Orchestra, he found his métier and lost a mint in dazzlingly adventurous opera and ballet seasons at Covent Garden, involving Diaghilev's Ballets Russes and similar expensive exotica. Narrowly avoiding bankruptcy, he flirted intermittently with the LSO – who would not tolerate his autocracy – and waited to be made music director of a symphony orchestra being formed by the BBC. When this plum position went to the unassuming Birmingham conductor Adrian Boult, Beecham petulantly formed a rival London Philharmonic Orchestra in 1932, enticing many of the country's finest players with fees beyond their dreams. Beecham claimed to have assembled the best band in the world. 'Nothing so electrifying has been heard in a London concert room for years,'[20] confirmed Ernest Newman in a *Sunday Times* review of the début.

Beecham's preferences were conspicuously un-English. He loathed Elgar's monumentalism and despised Vaughan Williams on many counts, packing his programmes instead with French and Russian delicacies and substituting the lightness of Haydn and Mozart for the *gravitas* of Beethoven and Brahms. He adored Delius and was the only conductor ever to make him sound like a composer of the very first rank. Beecham's sense of boyish fun atoned for misdemeanours that would have ruined a more responsible musician.

Boult, meanwhile, turned his BBC orchestra, the country's first salaried ensemble, into an outlet for daring modernities. He introduced concert performances of Alban Berg's *Wozzeck* and Ferruccio Busoni's *Doktor Faust*, operas that were heard on shortwave sets across central Europe and won respect for cultural standards on the offshore island. Boult established the principle – widely

Sir Thomas
Beecham.

Beecham – the elfin entrepreneur of half a century's musical activity.

Adrian Boult – creator of a broadcasting culture.

adopted in Europe and the British Empire – that public-service music broadcasting should contain an exceptionally well-rehearsed mixture of large-scale classics and rarefied new works that commercial ensembles dared not risk. The quality of his performances attracted Arturo Toscanini to give the seminal Beethoven cycles of the 1930s with the BBC Symphony Orchestra.

On the eve of war, Beecham abandoned his London Philharmonic and set off in fruitless pursuit of overseas glory. The orchestra resisted his advice to disband and played on throughout the war, overcoming the loss of its home and most of its instruments in the 1941 bombing of Queen's Hall. As soon as peace was restored, an EMI record producer, Walter Legge, envisaging a booming market for concert music, formed the Philharmonia to record standard repertoire with the celebrated German conductors Wilhelm Furtwängler, Otto Klemperer and Herbert von Karajan. Its repute quickly travelled from the record studio into the concert hall. Back in town and with no band of his own, Beecham founded yet another orchestra, the Royal Philharmonic, repeating the fail-safe device of offering munificent fees to the finest players.

From having no permanent orchestra at all, in forty years London had acquired five full-strength symphony ensembles and a host of smaller bands, more than any city could sensibly sustain. They could never give enough concerts to be financially viable, and relied for their existence on several other industries.

Recording had struck roots in London way back in the 1890s with the establishment of the Gramophone Company, His Master's Voice and Columbia. As technology turned electric and fidelity rose ever higher, famous artists began coming to London for the primary purpose of making records. Often they would schedule concerts around their sessions. Some, like Yehudi Menuhin, Alfred Brendel and Murray Perahia, made their home in the city.

HMV merged with Columbia to form EMI and founded a studio in a Victorian family house in Abbey Road, near Regent's Park. From the day of its inauguration by Edward Elgar and the LSO, with George Bernard Shaw squatting solemnly on the podium steps, Abbey Road entered the English language as a synonym for

Edward Elgar (centre top) and George Bernard Shaw (below) at the opening of Abbey Road studios.

record-making. Three decades later it turned into a tourist magnet after four young men posed for a cover photograph on its zebra crossing, emblem of the Beatles' 'Abbey Road' album.

In the record boom that followed the Second World War, American labels, unable to afford punitive union rates at home, would entice a London orchestra into the Abbey Road studio to play three sessions a day for a month on end, the musicians rarely seeing sunlight or their loved ones. The future conductor Neville Marriner, then a member of the LSO's second violins, recalls four such weeks of lucrative labour when the baton passed back and forth between the French conductor Pierre Monteux and the Hungarian Antal Dorati, producing an intensity of music-making that was 'nothing like the standardized performances of today'.[21]

In addition to recording symphonic pieces, orchestras were greatly in demand to provide backing for pop groups, make soundtracks for movies and play jingles for adverts. This least essential of consumer sectors was, however, subject to economic fluctuation and its worst crisis, set in motion by the Great Crash of 1929, saw the community of instrumental musicians in London cut by more than half.[22] The final catalyst in the city's musical ascendance arrived shortly afterwards, just when it was most desperately needed.

Britain was in the throes of severe economic depression when Adolf Hitler seized power in Germany, prompting thousands of Jews and political dissidents to flee, penniless, for their lives. By the end of 1937 some 5,500 had been admitted to the United Kingdom.[23] That number increased tenfold over the next two years, as Hitler annexed Austria and Czechoslovakia and menaced the rest of the Continent. Doctors and lawyers, musicians and actors, worked as factory hands and housemaids as they began to rebuild their lives in an alien country, whose language they mastered with difficulty and eccentricity. When war broke out, innate xenophobia was intensified by the rasp of their unmistakably German accents.

Concentrated in three or four suburbs north-west of the River Thames, the exiles found strength and reassurance in the musical culture which no tyrant or reluctant host was able to deny them. On Sunday afternoons, in Swiss Cottage and West Hampstead, shabby refugees would gather to play and listen to piano trios and sonatas, string quartets and song recitals, broken by a *Jause* (snack) interval for strong coffee and sugared biscuits. In the evenings, after work, they packed concert halls to the rafters, their life-and-death fervour altering England's habitual take-it-or-leave-it attitude towards culture. Half a century later the refugees and their descendants form a discernible core of the capital's concert society, and the names of Freud and Hofmannsthal, Mahler and Mendelssohn are still listed in the London telephone directory. A Sunday afternoon stroll through parts of NW6 will be accompanied by the strains of live chamber music filtering through heavy curtains and tightly shut windows.

London had welcomed colonies of refugees before, but none for whom culture (and music in particular) was as essential as food and shelter. Most of the displaced celebrities – Einstein, Schoenberg, Bartók, Thomas Mann – wound up unhappily in the United States. What Britain gained, however, was more durable than a clutch of household names. Many of the refugees were active musicians: composers, orchestral players, teachers, scholars, conductors and copyists. The amateurs among them played with near-professional proficiency and inculcated their children with a commensurate attachment to the art. They constituted an entire infrastructure of musical society, eager to contribute passion and expertise to their new homeland.

Their impact was instantaneous. In 1934 the ousted director of Berlin's state opera, Carl Ebert, joined forces with the former Dresden conductor, Fritz Busch, to form the finest little Mozart company in the world at John Christie's country house at Glyndebourne, on the rolling Sussex Downs. Rudolf Bing, their adjutant, formerly at Darmstadt and Berlin, went on after the war to found the Edinburgh summer festival in alliance with the exiled Viennese composer, Hans Gál.

Three publishers from Vienna, Ernst Roth, Erwin Stein and Alfred Kalmus, stirred up the trade with vigorous promotions of Berg, Bartók and Stravinsky. Universal Edition, the cutting-edge of Viennese modernism, was reinvented by Kalmus, who went on to discover and nurture the British talents of Harrison Birtwistle and Richard Rodney Bennett. Under Stein's aegis, Boosey & Hawkes, a rather dusty British imprint on the fringes of the West End, became an important trend-setter, pushing Benjamin Britten on to the world stage as the forerunner of an exciting new generation of British composers. Stein's daughter, Marion, was Britten's trusted friend; she married the Earl of Harewood, nephew of King George VI and a far-sighted opera administrator at Covent Garden and the English National Opera.

The former Berlin conductor, Walter Goehr, gave Michael Tippett his major break with the 1944 performance of *A Child of our Time*, an oratorio inspired by current events in Europe rather than by a traditional biblical topic. Goehr's son, Alexander, became a significant composer and Cambridge professor. Karl Rankl, formerly of the German Theatre in Prague, took charge of the Covent Garden orchestra after the war and raised it to international standard. Walter Bergmann, a lawyer by profession and baroque specialist by hobby, taught the British how to play Purcell. Max Rostal raised generations of string players at the Guildhall School; and three lads behind the barbed wire of an internment camp formed the nucleus of the world-famous Amadeus Quartet. The Frankfurt bibliophile, Paul Hirsch, donated his priceless music collection of 18,000 items to the British Museum, where it sat beside seminal music manuscripts collected by Stefan Zweig, the Austrian biographer and Strauss librettist. It would take a separate book to assess the full extent of the cultural and economic endowment that Hitler unwittingly bestowed upon Britain.

That is not to say that all were welcomed, and the composers in particular struggled for recognition against a current of chauvinist and reactionary critical opinion. When an opera competition for the 1951 Festival of Britain was won by three foreigners – Rankl, Berthold Goldschmidt and the Australian Arthur Benjamin – and by English communist Alan Bush, none of their works was allowed on stage. Instead, Covent Garden heard an insipid *Pilgrim's Progress* by the octogenarian Vaughan Williams. Goldschmidt, who for quarter of a century gave up composing in despair at local neglect, was in his late eighties before he received his first recording.

The worth of a creative artist is rarely immediately perceptible. Matyas Seiber's teachings of twelve-note technique took a generation or two to register among British composers, and his gruelling score for the BBC film of George Orwell's *Animal Farm* was years ahead of its time, though entirely apt for its subject. Perhaps the longest wait was endured by Schoenberg's Catalan pupil, Roberto Gerhard. Evicted from Spain by Franco's victory and from France by the advancing Germans, Gerhard scored wartime success on the BBC with folksy incidental music for *Don Quixote*. As soon as peace was restored he renounced all paid employment for two years to compose an opera on Robert Brinsley Sheridan's Spanish satire, *The Duenna*. Its atonal episodes were received with dismay at the BBC, while its tuneful songs and dances left the avant-garde aghast at a concert performance in Wiesbaden. More than half a century later, in January 1992, *The Duenna* was acclaimed in Madrid and Barcelona as the greatest Spanish opera of the century, although composed to an English text by an expatriate in Cambridge and London. Gerhard died without seeing his opera performed, but his Viennese wife, Poldi, lived to savour the triumph.

More refugees streamed in after the war, although hampered by ever-tighter immigration controls. Andrzej Panufnik, Poland's foremost composer, settled beside the Thames at Twickenham in 1954 and was ostracized for years by the British musical establishment for failing to adhere to a recognized school of composing. Czech and Hungarian musicians flocked to London after Soviet forces suppressed their freedom in 1956 and 1968. Year by year, newcomers added spice to a musical environment that grew all the time in courage and confidence. It was London that led the world's rediscovery of Mahler, with a 1960 centennial cycle of his symphonies, and of Janáček, with regular productions from the early 1950s. It gave simultaneous cycles of Schoenberg and Shostakovich that would have spelled box-office death in any other capital. It encouraged Leonard Bernstein and Aaron Copland when their reputations were at a low ebb. It gave a podium to Pierre Boulez when he could not work in Paris, and to Otto Klemperer when his career seemed to be over. As the Soviet Union disintegrated in 1991, musicians from various republics sought refuge, led by two leaders of the younger generation of Russian composers, Dmitri Smirnov and Elena Firsova. The Russian poetess, Irina Ratushinskaya, provided texts for a miniature concert masterpiece by Brian Elias, a London composer born in Bombay.

The evolution of music in London enjoyed an element of luck in the order in which the three Hs presented themselves. For without Henry Wood's improvement in playing standards, there would have been no room for recordings to develop, and without a viable concert life, the Hitler refugees would have despaired and fled. The vitality they generated was of a grass-roots validity that gave London the edge over its continental rivals. Where politicians in Paris and Berlin poured billions into self-aggrandizing showpiece festivals and buildings, London survived on the wits of its musicians and the fervour of its heterogeneous audience. By far the most attractive characteristic of music in London is its unspoken, and taken-for-granted, democracy.

2

THE VOID BETWEEN TWO ELIZABETHS

The blame for London's long musical silence until the present century lies, with a few notable exceptions, inescapably at the top. As far as music is concerned, the royal family has been either actively detrimental or indifferent to its progress. Few English rulers could ever sustain a tune, and none immersed himself in music as the Sun King did in Lully's compositions, or Joseph II of Austria in Mozart's operas, or Frederick the Great in his flute.

English sovereigns raised cathedrals to the greater glory of their own quasi-divinity, and from time to time patronized painters whose portraits assured them of iconographic posterity. Otherwise, they betrayed scant interest in matters spiritual or cultural.

The crowned heads of France and Frederick Barbarossa of Germany set off to save Jerusalem with an entourage of troubadours whose songs can still be heard today.[1] England's Richard the Lionheart, who was considered something of a minstrel-king, left only one slight tune to posterity – along with an apocryphal tale of his rescue from captivity by a devoted musician, Blondel de Nesle. This story gave rise to an interesting opera by André Grétry, but even credulous British scholars have conceded that 'Richard's reputation as poet and composer has been exaggerated.'[2]

While minnesingers, trouvères and premature polyphonists played in the courts of Europe, no musical stirring was noted in England until Edward I established a Chapel Royal to sing at his daily worship. Edward was a tyrant who massacred the Welsh, one of the world's most musical nations, and brutally expelled the Jews, traditional patrons of the arts. His sins were manifold and his need for musical consolation was doubtless little different from Hitler's.

A great composer arose in London in the fifteenth century. He

19

was snubbed by the Court and forced to seek employment else-where. John Dunstable obtained a position with the Queen of France, making advanced music that anticipated the Franco-Flemish style of Guillaume Dufay and Johannes Ockeghem. He left no appreciable mark on his native culture. Apart from the occasional fancy of a landed aristocrat and the newly formed guilds of city musicians, music in London might well have become extinct for all the monarchy cared.

As soon as Henry VII came to the throne, however, musical items began cropping up in the Household Records – payment for a song here, engagement of a viol consort there. Welsh by origin, the Tudors made music a matter of national importance. Henry VIII composed liberally in his youth. Thirty-four of his pieces survive in manuscript, though their quality is questionable. 'Never criticize the composition of a Royal Highness,' warned Brahms, 'you cannot know who wrote it.'[3] In Henry's case, there were at last better composers at Court than the uxoricidal king.

Henry's musical tastes were governed by the polygamous desires that prompted him to break with the Pope and invent a new strain of Christianity. His Anglican rite required devotional music. It was impartially supplied by composers who had previously decorated the Roman service. They had to tread warily in a theological minefield. The finest of them all, John Taverner, was actually arrested on charges of heresy. Rumour had it that he was released only on agreeing to betray fellow-musicians, a story that gave rise to a successful modern opera by Peter Maxwell Davies. There is no evidence that Taverner was a turncoat, though he may have accepted a few shillings from the secret service to report disloyal comments that he overheard on his travels around the country. He died in 1545, the founder of a formative English musical trinity with Christopher Tye and Thomas Tallis, who lived on through two further changes of religion, composing as diligently for Queen Mary's fiery reversion to Rome as for her sister Elizabeth's restoration of Anglicanism. It was not easy to be a composer under the Tudors, but you certainly could not say that it lacked variety.

Of Tye, all that is recorded is that he was a 'peevish and humoursome man' who, told by the Queen that he was playing out of tune, 'sent word to her that her ears were out of tune.'[4] Elizabeth was obviously tolerant of good musicians. Any other courtier would have paid heavily for such presumption. She did not hesitate to behead close friends who overstepped the mark, yet the keyboard master John Bull stumbled into the very sanctum of her virginal boudoir and escaped with an elegant apology, 'whereupon the queenes Maiesty was mollifyde and [she] sayd that so rayre a Bull hath songe as sweet as Byrd'.[5]

William Byrd was her favourite, although he made no secret of his unreformed Roman faith. Elizabeth awarded him, along with Tallis, a monopoly on music publishing and gave him lands confiscated from his co-religionists. Byrd and Tallis were among thirty musicians whom she employed;[6] with Bull, Alfonso Ferrabosco, Thomas Whythorne and Thomas Morley, their fame spread throughout the land and beyond. Christopher Hogwood has rightly pointed out that 'almost all examples of the art that we know from this period could more accurately be termed "London" than "English" music.'[7] The Queen was unquestioned patron of this remarkable renaissance and London was its breeding ground.

A brief flirtation with republicanism in the seventeenth century did not materially improve the capital's musicality. The Commonwealth of England was a puritanical régime suspicious of artistic frippery. Its Protector, Oliver Cromwell, shut the theatres, banned dancing and abolished music from religious worship.

The restoration of royalty came as a relief, bringing a sultry gust of hedonism, in which ladies exposed their bosoms, bawdiness returned to the language and the King's favourite mistress was a singing actress from Covent Garden, 'pretty, witty'[8] Nell Gwyn. Charles II had acquired French manners and morals during his

The patent granted by Elizabeth I to Tallis and Byrd.

THE EXTRACT AND EFFECT OF THE QVENES
Maiesties letters patents to Thomas Tallis and VVilliam Birde,
for the printing of musicke.

ELIZABETH by the grace of God Queene of Englande Fraunce and Irelande defender of the faith &c. To all printers bokesellers and other officers ministers and subiects greting, Knowe ye,that we for the especiall affection and good wil that we haue and beare to the science of musicke and for the aduauncement thereof, by our letters patents dated the xxii. of Ianuary in the xvii. yere of our raigne,haue graunted full priuiledge and licence vnto our welbeloued seruaunts Thomas Tallis and VVilliam Birde Gent. of our Chappell,and to the ouerlyuer of them, & to the assignes of them and of the suruiuer of them, for xxi.yeares next ensuing, to imprint any and so many as they will of set songe or songes in partes, either in English, Latine, French, Italian, or other tongues that may serue for musicke either in Churche or chamber, or otherwise to be either plaid or soonge,And that they may rule and cause to be ruled by impression any paper to serue for printing or pricking of any songe or songes, and may sell and vtter any printed bokes or papers of any songe or songes, or any bookes or quieres of such ruled paper imprinted, Also we straightly by the same forbid all printers bokesellers subiects & strangers, other then at is aforesaid, to do any the premisses, or to bring or cause to be brought out of any forren Realmes into any our dominions any songe or songes made and printed in any forren countrie,to sell or put to sale, vppon paine of our high displeasure, And the offender in any of the premisses for euery time to forfet to vs our heires and successors fortie shillings,and to the said Thomas Tallis & VVilliam Birde or to their assignes & to the assignes of the suruiuer of the,all & euery the said bokes papers songe or songes VVe haue also by the same willed & commaunded our printers,maisters & wardens of the misterie of stacioners,to assist the said Thomas Tallis and VVilliam Birde & their assignes for the dewe executing of the premisses.

exile. He flaunted them to a degree that caused a senior civil servant to fret that 'no good' would come 'to the State from having a prince so devoted to his pleasure'.[9]

This fear proved to be not without foundation. While Charles fiddled, the City of London burned to the ground (a Frenchman was sacrificially hanged for allegedly starting the fire) and a quarter of its populace died in the subsequent Great Plague. From the ashes, the astronomer Christopher Wren was given a royal warrant to reconstruct the city to an imaginative master-plan; most of his design was rejected by the citizenry and its centrepiece, St Paul's, had to be drastically modified.

On regaining the throne, Charles dispatched promising youths from the Chapel Royal to France and Italy to acquire style. Young Pelham Humfrey came back 'an absolute Monsieur', so contemptuous of all things English as 'would make a man piss',[10] but he died at twenty-six before his talent could truly flower. His pupil, Henry Purcell, reaped the benefits of his foreign education.

Charles appointed a Master of the King's Musick to take charge of his entertainment, inaugurating an unfortunate tradition. His first Master was a lutenist, painter and street-fighter, Nicholas Lanier by name. He was followed by a fraudulent Frenchman, Louis Grabu, who could not play any instrument. Ever since – apart from William Boyce and John Stanley in George III's reign – no active musician of merit has been Master of the King's or Queen's Musick. And incompetence gave way to sheer impotence when in 1893, the utterly forgettable Walter Parratt was appointed, ahead of Arthur Sullivan, Charles Stanford, Hubert Parry and a dozen others more reputable. By the time the title fell to Edward Elgar, he was too old to compose anything more than royal nursery suites. On his demise, Buckingham Palace picked the parochial Walford Davies, Parratt's pupil, ahead of Ralph Vaughan Williams or William Walton. A weary Arnold Bax became Master when, like Elgar, he was long past composing; he was succeeded by the innocuous Arthur Bliss, when Britten was the obvious choice. Since 1975 the incumbent has been Malcolm Williamson, an Australian who fell into disfavour when he failed to deliver the pieces required for ceremonial occasions. Would anyone in the House of Windsor notice if he submitted a previous fanfare written backwards?

Mad George III, ridiculed in the history books for losing the American colonies, was a notable exception to the rule of philistinism. Devoted to Handel, on whose knee he bounced as a child, he

George III, engorged.

preserved most of the great man's manuscripts and would quote stretches of *Messiah* in his daily conversations with the waving trees at Kew.

He raised monuments to mighty Handel, treated Haydn with respect and made his capital receptive to musical ideas. There was sadness in the theatre on the rare occasion that he missed an opera, for instance on the night 'news arrived in London of the decapitation of Louis XVI'.[11] He had an eye for a shapely soprano and his critical faculties were acute. Maurice Greene, the organist he inherited as Master of the King's Musick, was rightly dismissed as 'that wretched little crooked ill-natured insignificant writer player and musician'.[12] George III deserves a sweeter epitaph in music than Peter Maxwell Davies's cacophonous stage piece, *Eight Songs for a Mad King*.

Once George's son was proclaimed Regent, royalty returned to form, refusing to thank Beethoven for music honouring an English victory, let alone pay royalties for its performance. Ten years later the impoverished composer sent an obsequious, desperate invoice; this, too, elicited no response. The future George IV married off his pregnant mistress to the architect John Nash, whom he rewarded with a free hand in designing the glorious streets around Regent's Park. Beethoven, meanwhile, was cared for by the commoners of London's Philharmonic Society, which commissioned the ninth symphony.

Queen Victoria played the piano, was a fan of Mendelssohn's, received Wagner at Windsor and was forever urging Arthur Sullivan to write something serious for once, instead of those silly operettas. But, although cultured, she was never a patron of the arts. Her idle son and heir whiled away his evenings in the opera house, waking only to demand, 'Is it over yet?' Elgar wrote a second symphony in memory of Edward VII, an act of social aspiration rather than musical merit.

None of Edward's descendants has shown much interest in

Victoria and Albert go to the opera at Covent Garden.

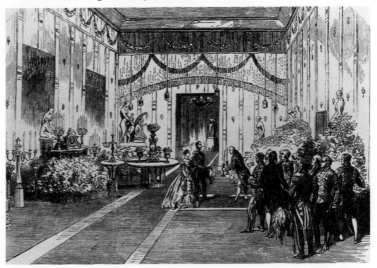

24

music, with the exception of the present heir to the throne, who played the cello as a boy and has campaigned for regressive trends in architecture and other arts. For his grandmother's ninetieth birthday he threw a concert at Buckingham Palace featuring three new pieces, two of them by the theatre composers Patrick Gower and Patrick Doyle and the third by David Matthews, a staid composer of middling age. A golden opportunity to shed limelight on unusually creative British composers was thereby squandered in an act of conservative caution. The Prince paid for only one of the pieces, the other two being commissioned by the cellist Mstislav Rostropovich and the Swiss conductor Paul Sacher. The music is eloquent enough, but scarcely stands as a monument to the lady it was meant to immortalize.

Charles's other interventions in musical life have been less benign. As president of the Philharmonia and English Chamber Orchestra, he does not hesitate to interfere when their interests are threatened. When the Philharmonia failed to win residency at the South Bank concert halls, Charles summoned the officials responsible in an attempt to secure a deal that would give his orchestra a larger slice of the cake. Given that the decision was the result of a proper democratic procedure, his action was irresponsible. This kind of dilettantish meddling has encouraged every orchestra in

Prince Charles picks up a pointer from conductor Colin Davis.

London to get itself a royal protector, in the hope of impressing government ministers and business sponsors. The lesser royals relate to 'their' orchestras as the Queen does to her racehorses: they make sure they are properly fed and cheer when they seem to be winning.

Politicians, too, have dabbled in patronage. Edward Heath took the title of president of the LSO without doing anything noticeable to justify his name on the notepaper. He liked to be asked to conduct, an activity that did nothing to raise public confidence in his executive abilities. Margaret Thatcher reserved her praise for foreign musical institutions that took no money from her privy purse; she liked to dine with conductors and openly envied their absolute power. John Major, married to the biographer of Joan Sutherland, regards free tickets to Covent Garden as one of the perks of office. Labour politicians, with the outstanding exception of Jennie Lee, the first Arts Minister, have had little time or inclination for the fripperies of fine art.

A form of snobbery no less virulent is visible behind the scenes where senior musicians jockey for a knighthood, which raises a man above his peers and makes his wife a Lady. The British honours system plays a pernicious role in the arts, rewarding favourite performers and public time-servers in astounding disproportion to the truly creative. It violates the tenth commandment by encouraging modest musicians to covet their neighbour's ermine. Edward Elgar went to his grave a bitter man, believing he had been unfairly denied elevation to the House of Lords. Benjamin Britten was the first musician to receive a peerage – slightingly, a *life* peerage that was granted as he lay dying. The establishment has many ways to make a man feel small. Ralph Vaughan Williams, to his credit, refused a knighthood on egalitarian socialist grounds and remained to the end of his days plain Doctor. Delius and Holst were the only other figures of consequence to escape the kiss of the monarch's sword, one saved by disreputability, the other by mortality. Harrison Birtwistle was tempted to decline but was discreetly advised that refusal would harm his public standing. A title that might have added lustre to the rise of British music has been devalued by its indiscriminate award to good composers and nonentities. At the same time, every director of a large music college, every principal conductor of a symphony orchestra and opera house, every chairman of a musical society with royal connections receives a knighthood as of right, regardless of art or merit. In democratic times, the act of patronage has reflected political acuity. Harold Wilson's government, wooing young voters, gave an MBE to the Beatles, supposedly for services to export.

There has been increasing cross-party consensus of the value of music as a diplomatic and commercial instrument. Labour abandoned its populist distaste for 'élitist' arts, and in 1988 a right-wing think-tank published an important survey revealing that investment in the arts generated hugely disproportionate profits in terms of increased tourism and foreign trade.[13] Music was oiling the wheels of the modern economy and the State was increasingly inclined to provide financial support, albeit on a much lower scale than in France or Germany. This political conversion is a recent phenomenon, for State funding began only in 1945, and in the early years a couple of thousand pounds was all an orchestra could expect. Today, two London orchestras receive more than a million pounds a year in public funding, and the Royal Opera House gets close to £19 million.

The principle of funding and the means of distribution were formulated in darkest wartime by the veteran economist John Maynard Keynes, a former Bloomsbury Group devotee married to a ballerina. His scheme provided for a national opera company, in place of the haphazard London seasons, along with support for artistically stimulating ideas from other institutions. Although heatedly contested at every spending round, the arts budget is now enshrined as securely as defence spending, and the Arts Council of Great Britain was given £220 million to disburse in the financial year 1992–3. The domestic audience for the arts in Britain is estimated to be 10 million, and many times that number experience the benefits of music in London on television, records and overseas concert tours.

If London has reached a pinnacle of musical success in the second Elizabethan era, its source is the same as it was in the time of the first Queen Elizabeth – the only other time in history when music thrived in London. Then, as now, artistic progress was the result of enlightened government subsidy. This is not to say that art cannot survive without political backing, but every young artist needs encouragement, and art in its entirety grows in confidence when it has the implicit support of the State and the nation.

Elizabethan values were rediscovered in 1910 when an English composer started his career at the late age of thirty-eight with a sonorous Fantasia for double string orchestra based on a Tudor score that he happened upon while editing some liturgical music. 'Vaughan Williams made the cardinal error of not including in all his compositions a theme by Thomas Tallis,'[14] carped Thomas Beecham. But the grand-nephew of Charles Darwin was adequately conditioned to survive unkind quips, and Vaughan Williams went on to earn worldwide fame from a Fantasia on Greensleeves adapted from an Elizabethan folk-song in his unremarkable Shakespearian opera, *Sir John in Love*. The Tudor chest he had broken open was quickly plundered by contemporaries. Percy Grainger tinkered with various tunes, and Peter Warlock made himself an authority on the epoch, whose dances he used in the *Capriol Suite*.

Later on, Benjamin Britten sensed personal affinities with the pensive, melancholy lutenist John Dowland, who, denied a position at Elizabeth's Court, was forced to wander in France and Denmark. Britten wrote an opera on the first Elizabeth for the coronation of the second in 1953. The trouble with *Gloriana* was not so much the music, which was elegantly neo-Elizabethan, but the tale of illicit relations between the Queen and her courtier, Essex, whom she beheaded as a traitor. The opera was deemed unsuitable for a royal occasion and has never been seen again at the Royal Opera House. Nevertheless, its creation drew an intriguing parallel between the two Elizabethan eras and others extended it across the musical spectrum.

The music of Dowland and Byrd came back into vogue. A hobbyist fascination with ancient instruments produced stirrings of an early music revival that revolutionized the performance of pre-classical music. Alfred Deller sang in a high counter-tenor voice unheard since the Renaissance. The London Consort of Viols simulated ancient performances. David Munrow preached and performed prehistoric music on primitive instruments as a scholarly cult became a commercial craze. Munrow committed suicide at thirty-three under the pressure of success, and his mantle was seized by Christopher Hogwood, John Eliot Gardiner, Trevor Pinnock and Roger Norrington, who rode to fame on what was in essence a tide of nostalgia for Elizabethan London.

The retrospective trend was equally contagious to composers who held that real music began in 1945 and that anything tuneful was inherently suspect. Maxwell Davies's *Taverner* was a noisy discourse on a moral dilemma that confronted artists in modern totalitarian states; Alexander Goehr's opera *Arden Must Die*, based on a Tudor play, was a political allegory 'about men and the man-

William Byrd, the great survivor.

ner in which they treat their fellow-men'[15] (the libretto was by Erich Fried, a Viennese poet living in Kilburn). The early stage works of Harrison Birtwistle, *Punch and Judy* and *Down by the Greenwood Side*, depicted the violent entertainments of Tudor times as paradigms of suppressed emotions.

Nor was neo-Elizabethanism locally confined. Igor Stravinsky chose for his first steps in twelve-note writing a cantata on Elizabethan songs; Leonard Bernstein scored his greatest hit with *West Side Story*, an updated Shakespearean love-tragedy; Shostakovich wrote music for *Hamlet*.

There is no ready explanation for this far-reaching reversion to an era whose values and habits are so alien to our own. One might understand composers turning for gaiety to the Restoration, or for moral certainty to Victorian England, but the fratricidal and sanguinary Tudor period has little to offer – beyond the fertility of its arts. In the imagination of modern composers, this sufficed to conjure up the romantic ideal of a model society in which creators cross-pollinated in a pre-Wagnerian *Gesamtkunstwerk*, a union of all the arts.

In Elizabethan London, theatre, music, poetry and painting flourished in feverish intimacy. Composers of the Chapel Royal wrote tunes for the popular plays of Shakespeare, Ben Jonson and Christopher Marlowe; the Queen herself supported the new commercial theatres against objections by the city fathers. The theatrical scene-painter Inigo Jones designed palaces for her successor, James I. Jones combined with Ben Jonson to invent a medley of music, drama and dance known as the masque, a precursor of opera. Playwrights sang madrigals, architects wrote poetry, dancers directed stage plays.

This interaction of the arts lasted throughout the next century, despite civil war and cultural oppression by the Puritans. The poet Milton, son of a musician, produced masques with various composers. The composer Purcell, supplementing his court and church incomes, found an appreciative public in the theatre and an eminent partner in the poet John Dryden, who hid from his creditors in the composer's room in the clock-tower of St James's Palace, 'where he was perfectly safe, and could moreover enjoy the air and exercise in the Palace gardens'.[16] An English style of opera was briefly envisaged. It came to an end in the decade after Purcell's death, when no composer in London was remotely the equal of its literary writers. A revival could not begin until music regained the upper hand.

The surge of indigenous composers and European influence in the late twentieth century finally created the appropriate conditions. In the past two decades, the playwright Edward Bond has written political pieces with the German composer, Hans Werner Henze. The science fiction of Doris Lessing struck a chord with the American minimalist, Philip Glass. Tom Stoppard devised a satire on Soviet psychiatry to music by André Previn. Harrison Birtwistle, the most unyielding of British composers, combined with Tony Harrison, the craggiest of poets, in *Yan Tan Tethera*, a television opera for sheep and singers. At the National Theatre, where he was director of music, Birtwistle applied a laconic wit in arranging Mozart's music for Peter Shaffer's world-sweeping *Amadeus*.

Other arts sought to collaborate with London's music as it recovered its self-respect. Shakespearian stage directors like Peter Hall and Jonathan Miller turned to opera in a manner unthinkable only a generation before, when Peter Brook was turfed out of Covent Garden for daring to commission Salvador Dali's scenery for *Salome*. Nowadays David Hockney's colourful settings sell an opera as surely as any of its divas, and some of the delight of Oliver Knussen's children's opera, *Where the Wild Things Are*, derives from its design by the brilliant book-illustrator, Maurice Sendak.

The enrichment of opera contributed in turn to the rebirth of musical theatre in the West End, directed with operatic depth by the likes of Peter Hall and Trevor Nunn (*Cats*). The debt owed by Andrew Lloyd Webber to operatic scores and stories is self-evident. London's hit musicals now take their cue from opera instead of Broadway. When *Les Misérables* transferred to Vienna, critics quickly perceived its Wagnerian undertones. The commercial theatre for which London has been justly famed since Shakespeare's day is increasingly reliant for ideas on the activities of London's concert halls and opera companies.

Why music in London should have lingered so long as the weakling of the arts, why local composers were so cowed and unconfident that Byron and the Brontës looked to continental musicians for inspiration, is cause for much patriotic soul-searching. The historical facts, though, are incontrovertible. Once the last echoes of Elizabethan fecundity were buried in poor Purcell's grave and State support withered, English music became a wasteland for two centuries, ripe for foreign exploitation.

3

BENEATH A GIANT SHADOW

Imagine what might have happened if Bach came to England and Handel stayed at home. The unassuming Leipzig cantor would quietly churn out concertos and cantatas for St Paul's, teaching counterpoint to its choristers and founding a solid tradition on which posterity could build. Within the space of two generations, little Haydns and Mozarts start sprouting in Birmingham and Leicester, a Beethoven is born in Tunbridge Wells. Back in Germany, meanwhile, musical progress is paralysed by the towering figure of Handel. For a hundred years no one dares compose anything but oratorios, and every new talent is axiomatically deemed his inferior. Orchestras are reduced to importing composers from England.

A preposterous hypothesis? Not entirely, for Germany's musical rise is mirrored in Britain's decline, and both share roots in the *annus mirabilis* of 1685, when Bach and Handel came into the world. London at that moment was, despite nervous tension over rekindled Catholicism at court, a hive of musical activity. Its theatres thrived and regular concerts evolved, ahead of the rest of Europe, when the violinist John Banister quit the Chapel Royal, took a room over a tavern in White Fryers, 'made a raised box for the musitians, whose modesty required curtaines',[1] and presented daily 'Musick performed by Excellent Masters, beginning at four of the Clock in the afternoon'.[2] One shilling was the price of admission and 'call for what you please' from the bar.

Catering to a slightly more sophisticated clientele, a coal merchant, Thomas Britton, set up a concert room above his store – 'with a window but very little bigger than the Bunghole of a Cask ... where any Body that is willing to take a hearty Sweat may have the pleasure of hearing many notable Performances'.[3] Banister's enterprise earned him a tomb in Westminster Abbey, Britton's a wall-space in the National Portrait Gallery. Around the same time, in the well-watered Islington garden of a surveyor called Sadler, summer music mingled with grosser pastimes as the resident buffoon consumed a live cat, an 11-year-old urchin danced licentiously and:

> ... Musick's charms in lulling sounds
> Of Mirth and harmony abounds;
> While nymphs and swains with beaux and belles
> All praise the joys of *Sadler's Wells*.[4]

Another room for concerts was being built on Villiers Street off the Strand. With nightly entertainments at Court and at the ducal mansions, London now offered more music to a wider public than any other city. Berlin, by comparison, was a composer-less backwater with no serious music to be heard outside church; Vienna was busy fighting off the Turks. Paris danced to Lully's libidinous fiddle and Rome adored the archangelic Corelli, himself a Purcell fan. While French and Italian styles predominated, a distinctly English musical genre was becoming discernible.

The death of Purcell in 1695 put paid to all that, removing at the Mozartian age of thirty-five a source of fertility that held sway over all forms of creation, from theatre music to church, from advanced sonatas to simple songs. His loss to melody was incalculable, to English music irreparable. 'Oh, go to te teffel [sic],' Handel would snarl at the suggestion decades later that his oratorio *Jephtha* had Purcellian echoes. 'If Purcell had lived, he would have composed better music than this.'[5]

The surviving composers were inadequate to fill Purcell's void and, just as a new generation was finding its voice, along came Handel and crushed its confidence stone cold. The Elector of Hanover's Kapellmeister was twenty-five and a star in Italy when he prospected London in 1711 with an opera, *Rinaldo*, strung together in a couple of weeks from bits of earlier scores. The aristocratic audience, avid for Italian singing, instantly recognized Handel's superiority over Neapolitan opera-makers like Giovanni Bononcini. Only when malice outshone melodic appreciation was his primacy ever questioned:

Some say, compar'd to Bononcini
That Mynheer Handel's but a ninny;
Others aver that to him Handel
Is scarcely fit to hold a candle.
Strange, all this difference should be
'Twixt Tweedledum and Tweedledee![6]

Rinaldo was published in London by John Walsh, earning its composer a fortune of £1,500. Handel was given leave to return the following year and remained in London, barring excursions, for the rest of his long life. Coming from a country where composers

Mighty Handel.

were treated as court jesters or church slaves, he found that England offered him both social status and the opportunity to make real money.

When the Hanoverian Elector became King George I, Handel shrugged off the bonds of formal employment and pursued his craft autonomously in a city that offered numerous alternatives to an imaginative entrepreneur. Snubbed at Court, he entertained the nobility. Spurned by fickle duchesses, he turned to the business classes. When the bottom fell out of opera, he invented oratorio. When singing palled, he gave open-air concerts at the Vauxhall pleasure gardens and organ recitals at the Abbey. On Sundays he played, unpaid, at his own parish church in Hanover Square. Introduced to an expanding community of resettled Jewish exiles from Inquisition-ridden Spain, he gave them heroes in *Joshua*, *Judas Maccabaeus* and *Esther*, broad-minded gifts from a devoutly Christian composer. He was happy to adapt to social and cultural change, demanding only that his music, once written, was properly respected.

In all matters pertaining to his art, he had the arrogance of genius and a tolerance to match. He withheld his ire from no one, hurling kettledrums at a miscreant musician and obliging even royalty to retreat murmuring, 'Hush! Handel's in a passion!'[7] The reverend librettist of *Judas Maccabaeus*, venturing to suggest that some music might not fit the text of a proposed aria, was driven from the house with the cry, 'What! you teach me Music? It is your words is bad. Hear the passage again. There! Go you, make words to that Music.'[8]

A huge man, of awesome appetites for food and drink (though seemingly asexual), Handel terrorized mere mortals with a voice that 'was very formidable indeed'[9] and a manic-depressive disposition that earned him the nickname of 'Great Bear'. He was grizzly, 'impetuous, rough and peremptory in his manners',[10] and once threatened to throw the soprano, Francesca Cuzzoni, through an upper-storey window if she failed to sing every note he had written.

But he lacked malice and his rage was readily appeased; 'when he *did* smile, it was his sire the sun bursting out of a black cloud',[11] wrote the music historian Charles Burney. Capable of impetuous acts of generosity, Handel donated the manuscript of *Messiah* to the Foundling Hospital for abandoned children and raised £7,000 – equivalent to a quarter of a million pounds in current terms – by means of charity performances.

The structure erected for Handel's Music for the Royal Fireworks.

So vivid and vast a personality could not fail to leave its mark on a world wider than music. Political writers recounted his doings as thinly veiled satires of government scandals. Poets peppered him with verses. Statues were erected in his own lifetime – the most numerous and faithful by the Frenchman, Louis-François Roubiliac – and his music was actually debated in Parliament.

Overcome by *Messiah*, the King stood up at the words 'For the Lord God omnipotent reigneth' in the Hallelujah chorus, raising the entire audience to its feet in a custom frequently observed in England to this day. 'I should be sorry if I only entertained them,' remarked Handel, when congratulated on his oratorio. 'I wish to make them better.'[12]

Aspirations of this magnitude went far beyond the prescribed role of a composer to divert and delight. It set Handel apart from his art, placing him among the living immortals as, blind and pain-ridden, he thundered from the organ keyboard in *Samson* like a tortured prophet. Having vanquished two generations of would-be rivals, he died supreme. Christoph Willibald von Gluck, inventor of modern opera, hung Handel's portrait over his bed so that his was the first face he saw each morning. Haydn, father of the symphony, broke down in the Hallelujah chorus sobbing, 'He is the master of us all!'[13], and Beethoven proclaimed him 'the greatest composer that ever lived'.[14]

In Britain he was above criticism – George III saw to that, censoring Burney's Handel essays to ensure their probity. The composer William Boyce perceived the eclecticism in Handel's repeated borrowings from other men's music and elegantly turned intellectual theft into a virtue. 'He takes pebbles and converts them to diamonds,'[15] marvelled Boyce, proceeding to model his own compositions on the master's.

Lesser musicians were stultified into silence or feeble simulation. The tale is told of Maurice Greene who took a solo anthem to Handel for his approval. The two friends would strip to the waist as they played for pleasure far into the summer's night on the organ at St Paul's, gorging themselves afterwards at a neighbouring hostelry. Next morning, when Greene demanded a reaction to his anthem, Handel pointed vaguely outside.

'I think it vanted air, Dr Greene,' he said, in Teutonic brogue.

'Air, Sir?' asked his friend.

'Yes, air; and so I did hang it out of de window.'[16]

The gargantuan Handel commemoration at Crystal Palace.

Such contempt for the efforts of his colleagues, combined with royal and popular adulation, obliged British musicians for the next century-and-a-half to abase themselves in Handel's shadow. A Victorian composer could write nothing worthier than oratorio. Orgies of Handolatry were indulged in public places, beginning with the Westminster Abbey commemorations ordered by George III, and reaching a grinding climax in the 1885 bicentennial *Messiah* belted out by 4,500 performers for a crowd of nearly 88,000 at Crystal Palace.

Handel had converted England to a musical monotheism that allowed the worship of only one composer at a time, preferably a German. Of the flurry of composers who followed his trail, none came near to replacing him.

François André Philidor of France was the next to take up residence, earning his keep as chess champion in the coffee-houses around Charing Cross. 'I am not surprised, Sir, that in England all doors should be closed to a great musician and open to a famous chess-player,'[17] griped the dictionarist Denis Diderot, begging his friend to return home and write more operas. But Philidor was playing simultaneous games in blindfold, and failed to notice when the Reign of Terror cut him off from Paris and his loved ones.

'On Monday last,' reported the newspapers of 2 September 1795, 'Mr Philidor, the celebrated chess player, made his last move, into the other world.'[18]

The London Bach made a more lasting impression. Johann Christian, eleventh and youngest son of the late cantor of Leipzig, came to write operas for the King's Theatre in 1762 and procured a post as music master to the German-born Queen Charlotte. In this capacity, he was soon called in to examine an 8-year-old visiting prodigy, Wolfgang Amadeus Mozart.

The two musicians struck sparks off one another and enjoyed a mutual respect until Bach's early death, mourned by Mozart in the slow movement of his twelfth piano concerto (K.414). The Mozarts spent fifteen months in London, during which time the boy wrote his first symphony. Bach made his home in the city, marrying an Italian soprano and cultivating a cheery circle of artist friends. The painter Thomas Gainsborough, who twice did his portrait, sorely tried Bach's patience by dabbling at Purcell and Byrd on the keyboard, until Bach pushed him from the seat crying, 'Now dat is too bad; dere is no law by goles! why the gompany is to listen to your murder of all these ancient gombosers.'[19] Gainsborough's dilet-

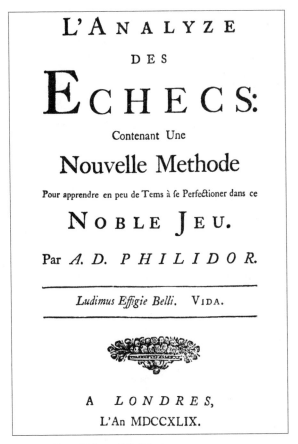

L'ANALYZE

DES

ECHECS:

Contenant Une

Nouvelle Methode

Pour apprendre en peu de Tems à ſe Perfeƈtioner dans ce

NOBLE JEU.

Par *A. D. PHILIDOR.*

Ludimus Effigie Belli. VIDA.

A LONDRES,

L'An MDCCXLIX.

Frontispiece of Philidor's magnum opus.

tante passion, though, was symptomatic of a spreading interest in music; the painter was forever pestering his son-in-law, the oboist Johann Christian Fischer, to teach him a new instrument. A century later, the portraitist John Singer Sargent was similarly obsessive in his passion for playing Fauré, Grainger and Albéniz.[20]

Bach died in 1782 at forty-six leaving a pile of debts, some engaging operas, symphonies and concertos, and two lasting legacies. Together with his compatriot Carl Friedrich Abel, he had inaugurated the world's first series of subscription concerts, consisting mainly of music by the two promoters but laying the foundation for an annual concert season. It was a cut above the *ad hoc* entertainments of borrowed bar-rooms and summer gardens, and success spurred them on to build their own concert hall on the corner of Hanover Square and Hanover Street, next to Oxford Circus. Each invested £5,000, with the remaining £10,000 coming from a Swiss dancing master, Giovanni Gallini. This proved financially ruinous for the composers, who were bought out cheaply by Gallini, but it provided an 800-seat hall for modern concerts, the perfect place for Joseph Haydn to be introduced with twelve symphonies he had written specially for London.

At a loose end in Vienna, his orchestra having lately disbanded, Haydn was accosted by a German-born violinist from the Covent Garden theatre, Johann Peter Salomon, with the greeting: 'I am Salomon of London and have come to fetch you.'[21] Bidding farewell to Mozart, whom he never saw again, the modest Kapellmeister of Esterháza crossed Europe to find himself famed in a world capital. 'Everyone wants to know me,'[22] he exclaimed in astonishment.

'The sight of that renowned composer so electrified the audience as to excite an attention and pleasure superior to any that had ever, to my knowledge, been caused by instrumental music in England,' wrote Burney. 'All the slow movements were repeated,

'Papa' Haydn, father of twelve London Symphonies.

which never before happened, I believe, in any country.'[23]

'Like our own SHAKSPEARE [sic],' hyperbolized the *Morning Chronicle*, 'he moves and governs the passions at his will.'[24]

Haydn's sexagenarian passions were moved and governed by a neighbourly widow, Rebecca Schroeter, with whom, his diaries indicate, he enjoyed moments sweeter than any granted by his shrewish wife and grasping mistress. Haydn had a delightful time in London, attended the Lord Mayor's banquet and the races at Ascot, received a doctorate from Oxford, was painted by Sir Joshua Reynolds and fêted by George III. His diary, recorded with the wide-eyed wonder of an innocent abroad, is a catalogue of trivia – the stranger's foot under the Duchess of Devonshire's petticoat, a recipe for rum cocktail, statistics of 22,000 deaths in London in 1791, 800,000 annual cartloads of coal consumed and 'a fog so thick one might have spread it on bread'.[25]

His twelve London Symphonies, the most sprightly of his 104, bubble with imagination and incident. The *Surprise* (No. 94) catches listeners unawares in a quiet passage with a thunderous drumbeat; the *Miracle* (No. 96) gives thanks for his audience's salvation when a chandelier came crashing down; while the *Military* (No. 100) proved the most popular of his entire output.

He had passing rivals for public attention in the pianists Muzio Clementi and Jan Dussek and in the 14-year-old prodigy Johann Nepomuk Hummel, whose vogue inspired the limerick:

> There was a young lady of Rio
> Who essayed to play Hummel's *Grand Trio*
> Her skill was so scanty
> She played it *andante*
> Instead of *allegro con brio*.[26]

But Papa Haydn was untroubled by the success of others, or by Handel's shadow. He witnessed the annual Handel commemoration of 1791 from a seat near the royal box and 'was struck as if he had been put back to the beginning of his studies and had known nothing up to that moment'.[27]

He had no wish to change the world as Handel did and behaved as a perfect guest in London, giving offence to no one and moving none of the artistic furniture. In two 18-month visits he earned the equivalent of twenty-four years' wages at Esterháza and returned home with enough money for his old age. Once, on his way back to

Vienna, he stopped in Bonn to pick up a pupil who had agreed to be Haydn's assistant on his next London trip. But the plan fell through, and Ludwig van Beethoven never reached England.

After the Napoleonic Wars, Beethoven was repeatedly invited by the Philharmonic Society, formed by Salomon and friends in 1813 to reverse the wartime decline of orchestral music. Several of its emissaries appeared on Beethoven's doorstep and were warmly received. 'He is very desirous to come to England,'[28] remarked Sir George Smart, after reporting to Beethoven on the London première he had conducted of the ninth sympathy, which the Society commissioned. Learning that the composer was destitute, the Society sent him £100 'to be applied to his comforts and necessities'.[29] And eight days before he died, Beethoven sent fresh metronome markings for the Ninth, with a promise of finer things to come: 'May heaven only restore my health soon and I shall show those magnanimous Englishmen how greatly I appreciate their sympathy for my sad fate.'[30] But the anticipated tenth symphony was unfinished and remained unheard for 160 years until its première by the still-functioning Philharmonic Society in a version reconstructed from fragments by an Aberdeen musicologist, Barry Cooper.

Beethoven was virtually the last great composer never to visit London. The only subsequent absentees were Schubert, who had no lifetime international reputation, Schumann, who was too inept a performer to be invited, and Brahms, who stubbornly resisted. Brahms had 'an exaggerated notion of the inflexibility of English social laws', surmised his English pupil, Florence May. 'In England it always rains, rains, rains and in England one always has to wear evening dress,'[31] he told another admirer. He was terrified of sea-sickness and called himself, in an apologetic letter to British friends, 'a ponderous stick-in-the-mud'.[32]

Every other notable composer stayed in London, and many made it their second home. Showmen like Paganini and Liszt used it as a base while they criss-crossed the British Isles and mesmerized its womenfolk, some of whom proved memorably pliant. Bellini and Donizetti imported bel canto opera, after Rossini had been sumptuously received then nearly expelled for singing to the King in a simulated castrato shriek.

Rossini's celebrity eclipsed poor Carl Maria von Weber, who came to earn a crust for his family by creating *Oberon* at Covent Garden. Sixteen laborious rehearsals produced an ephemeral success and his benefit concert clashed calamitously with the races at

Epsom. On the morning of 5 June 1826, in Sir George Smart's house at 91 Great Portland Street, the composer of *Der Freischütz* was found dead in bed, with tubercles the size of breakfast eggs choking his ravaged lungs. He was buried at Moorfield's Chapel to the sound of Mozart's *Requiem*, but was not allowed to rest in peace. Seventeen years later, his remains were exhumed on the orders of Richard Wagner, Kapellmeister at Dresden, and at no small expense repatriated. He was reburied with a Wagnerian eulogy: 'Behold, the Briton does you justice, the Frenchman admires you, but only the German can *love* you!'[33]

Wagner came to London in 1839 to pay homage at the house where Weber died and to approach the historical novelist Sir Edward Bulwer-Lytton, MP, whose *Rienzi* he was composing. Lytton was out of the town, as was Smart, to whom he had sent an unsolicited *Rule, Britannia!* overture. The Philharmonic Society turned it down because its theme 'is here considered common place'[34] and, since Wagner could not afford to pay return postage, the score was sent to the British Library, where it remains.

Altogether it was an abortive, expensive 8-day trip for the 26-year-old musician. He stayed with his wife, Minna, and their huge dog, Robber, at the King's Arms in Old Compton Street, rode his first train, endured 'a ghastly London Sunday' and, after hearing debates at both Houses of Parliament, reckoned he 'knew all there was to know about the capital of Great Britain'.[35]

One salient fact did not escape him. Its presiding musical genius was his abominated antipode – the cosmopolitan Felix Mendelssohn, who aroused Wagner's envy as the dominant figure in his own birthplace, Leipzig. Exquisitely well-spoken in English, adored by the young Queen Victoria, Mendelssohn combined the manners of a gentleman with panache as a composer, conductor and pianist. In English eyes, he was the equal of Beethoven – George Grove gave them similar space in his dictionary – and, despite obvious disparities in character, a second Handel. He played the organ of every chapel he entered like a man possessed and his oratorios *St Paul* and *Elijah* were deemed the modern equivalent of *Messiah*.

To the Philharmonic Society that had failed to entice Beethoven, Mendelssohn was a tremendous catch. Ravished by his début in Beethoven's Emperor Concerto, they made him an honorary member and commissioned his Italian Symphony for a modest fee. Mendelssohn was eminently reasonable in all his dealings, business or social – so reasonable that his nervous collapse and death at thirty-eight form a puzzling and abrupt coda to an unusually well-ordered existence. 'This is what always seemed questionable to me about Mendelssohn,' reflected Wagner in an objective moment, 'that he never lost control of himself.'[36]

Deeply attached to his German Fatherland,[37] Mendelssohn made ten trips to England. He manipulated its levers of influence through London-based friends such as the pianist Ignaz Moscheles and a stream of performing emissaries, who included the remarkable violinists Ferdinand David and Joseph Joachim. He steered public taste towards classically sanitized performances of Beethoven and Schumann and away from the wilder shores of Liszt and romanticism. A generation of British composers, from William Sterndale Bennett to Arthur Sullivan, were schooled in Mendelssohn's Leipzig.

Joachim returned to London year in, year out, for six decades.

Felix Mendelssohn.

The pianist Clara Schumann, when her husband subsided into insanity, became another fixture. Together, they invented a Mendelssohn succession that embraced Schumann and his protégé, Brahms, whose songs were printed in England as early as 1854.

'Mendelssohn at least had some ideas,' scorned Wagner, 'then came Schumann, a brooding fool, and now Brahms with nothing at all.'[38] The struggle for supremacy in German music was to be waged on English soil. Exiled from Germany for revolutionary sedition, Wagner was brought to London in 1855 to conduct the Philharmonic Society as a counter-attraction to Hector Berlioz, who was hired by rebels at the New Philharmonic. The rivals got on warily well, though Berlioz pleased the critics – who defiantly supported him when the public hissed *Benvenuto Cellini* at Covent Garden – while Wagner was taken to task for his attacks on the saintly Mendelssohn. 'A desperate charlatan' the *Sunday Times* called him. 'Herr Wagner is a necessary evil,' commented the *Morning Post*. 'Germany, however, and not England, is the proper arena for his exploits.'[39]

He returned once more, two decades later, aiming to recoup losses from the Bayreuth *Ring* at eight mass concerts in the Royal Albert Hall. Over the years, Liszt had helped make him respectable and the conductor Edward Dannreuther formed a London Wagner Society to advance his cult, particularly among a growing colony of German mercantile immigrants. *Lohengrin* was the first of his operas to reach Covent Garden and *Tannhäuser* was something of a hit, when sung in Italian.

Wagner's physical presence in 1877 served to rally support. The novelist George Eliot and poet William Morris were much impressed; Edward Burne-Jones painted a famous portrait; the Queen summoned him to Windsor. The critics were receptive and his assistant, Hans Richter, conducted so capably that a consortium of music-lovers engaged him for annual concerts at St James's Hall. Richter returned annually for the rest of the century, striking a judicious balance in his seasons between Wagner and Brahms. The younger generation was infatuated with Wagner, and a 20-year-old critic called George Bernard Shaw wasted no opportunity to extol him at Brahms's expense. London staged its first *Ring* cycle in 1882, before any other capital city except Munich, Vienna and Berlin. A second *Ring*, under Gustav Mahler's direction, was staged in 1892.

The Mendelssohn lobby, however, remained paramount, with Bennett and Grove heading the two music colleges and despatching their star graduates to finishing schools at Leipzig and Frankfurt, where Clara Schumann held court. The retired soprano Jenny Lind and her husband Otto Goldschmidt, both Mendelssohn protégés, kept up the oratorios and the standards of musical propriety. Brahms was adulated *in absentia,* and any symphonist, like Antonin Dvořák, who came bearing his commendation was assured of a welcome and a commission from the Philharmonic Society. Shaw, a lone sniper who winged Brahms by indicting him with Gladstonian verbosity ('which outfaces its own commonplaceness by dint of sheer magnitude'),[40] swore that he would rather die than hear Dvořák's *Requiem* again, 'since the penalty of default did not exceed death'.[41] Wagner, in Shaw's reviews, was referred to as the 'Meister' and no hint of fallibility was admitted in his works and thought.

British composers were, on the whole, befuddled by the clash of Teutons and aimed for harmless neutrality. Arthur Sullivan was torn between lampooning Wagner in his operettas and echoing him in attempts at epic opera. Charles Villiers Stanford and Hubert Parry, joint captains of England's symphonic cricket team, achieved a tacit compromise by which Parry bowled like Wagner while Stanford emulated Brahms – so fervently on one occasion that a theme in his Irish Symphony was identical to a passage in Brahms's unpublished Fourth. Hans Richter offered impartial encouragement and gave British symphonies a flattering concert outlet in Berlin. It was Richter who sounded the resurrection of English music with a performance of Edward Elgar's Variations on an Original Theme (Enigma) which, on 19 June 1899, ended two centuries of creative insufficiency and instilled a new generation with the confidence to compose.

Elgar was not much of a model for original creators. His eclecticism was audible in every work. Mendelssohn's *Calm Sea and Prosperous Voyage* was quoted at the heart of the Enigma, while Schumann, Gounod, Brahms and Saint-Saëns were audible in the two symphonies and concertos. The son of a small shopkeeper, uneasy in high society, an anguished Catholic among casual Anglicans, he took his cue from continental trends that flourished in London as its trading importance increased. Puccini and Verdi were hugely popular at the dawn of the century, as were Grieg and Tchaikovsky. Sibelius emerged as the symphonist to simulate. Yet the strongest undercurrent in the rebirth of English music was an *entente cordiale* with France. Ever since the Franco-Prussian War chased Napoleon III and Charles Gounod to London as refugees, a musical bond had formed between the neighbours as an antidote to German power. Saint-Saëns wrote the most durable of his symphonies for London, and Gabriel Fauré arrived with charming incidental music for Maurice Maeterlinck's symbolist play, *Pelléas et Mélisande*. Debussy, forced to retreat from a Parisian love-tangle, crossed the Channel to compose *La Mer*.

Ralph Vaughan Williams went to Paris as a mature student to seek instruction from Maurice Ravel. Frederick Delius settled at Grez-sur-Loing and copied the impressionists. Lennox Berkeley led a thin stream of pupils to Nadia Boulanger. Benjamin Britten set poems by Victor Hugo and Paul Verlaine while in his final term at prep school. Nevertheless, the grip of tradition scarcely slackened and there was no surer way for a new composer to find favour than with an oratorio in the Handel and Mendelssohn mould – as William Walton demonstrated in 1931 with *Belshazzar's Feast*. Every year until 1939 the Royal Albert Hall was rocked by Samuel Coleridge-Taylor's *Hiawatha*, sung by choirs charabanced in from every corner of the land. The dominant triumvirate of twentieth-century modernism, Arnold Schoenberg, Igor Stravinsky and Béla Bartók, made scant impact on the music that was composed in London either before or after the Second World War.

Claude Debussy photographs La Mer.

47

All three paid frequent visits, but their local acolytes lacked clout in a culture that remained stubbornly attached to nostalgic pastoralities and the models of two centuries before.

That grip was finally eased by a charismatic Frenchman who aimed to replace Handel's stranglehold with his own strictures. Pierre Boulez, the Parisian firebrand who threatened to burn down opera houses, was introduced to London by a new regime at the BBC that was giving the nation a forcible baptism in contemporary sounds. William Glock, as controller of music, was wedded to music that was cerebrally conceived and intentionally abstruse. Boulez proclaimed that any living composer who failed to assimilate serial rigorisms and electronic technologies was unworthy of performance. He particularly abhorred Britten, as a man who wasted his talent on conservatism.

As chief conductor of the BBC Symphony Orchestra, Boulez refused to conduct Tchaikovsky or Mozart. He moved concerts into such unusual venues as an unconverted railway shed in Camden Town, sat his predominantly youthful audiences on the floor and debated with them far into the night on the merits of the music he had just conducted. His was a necessary corrective to the blanket of convention that was threatening to stifle concert life under the patrician conductor Malcolm Sargent, with a carnation in his buttonhole. As well as introducing a gamut of alien influences, Boulez brought to the fore a generation of British radicals, centred upon the Manchester-schooled cartel of Harrison Birtwistle, Alexander Goehr and Peter Maxwell Davies. Others flocked to his Parisian dungeon, the IRCAM centre for discovering and promoting a new language of sound. At least one British masterpiece, Jonathan Harvey's *Mortuos plango, vivos voco*, was conceived at IRCAM, as was the electronic music for Birtwistle's opera, *The Mask of Orpheus*, which no less a critic than the pianist Alfred Brendel considered the finest English opera since Purcell's. Three decades' worth of composers, from Richard Rodney Bennett to George Benjamin, sought Boulez's tutelage and patronage.

Boulez was engagingly open about his objectives and the methods by which he meant to achieve them. 'In politics, you call this entryism,'[42] he said, describing his pursuit of power. In addition to the positions he occupied, he lobbied on behalf of allies like John Drummond as music chief at the BBC and Nicholas Snowman, his IRCAM administrator, who was appointed general director of arts on the South Bank in 1985.

Yet, despite his enormous charisma and the best efforts of his supporters, Boulez failed to achieve the conformity he preached. This was due, in part, to a creative cul-de-sac in which he found himself amid a late-century return to eternal verities, which exposed avant-garde ideologies as chimerical. Boulez has not completed a major score since *Répons* in 1981 and has been under increasing pressure to justify his pontifications in Paris, where his writ still holds sway. His painful medicine weaned London of its last shred of devotion to massed oratorios but failed to convert it to ascetic modernism.

For Boulez had come on to a scene enriched by the Elgarian renaissance and fortified by the universal achievements of Benjamin Britten and the rugged individualisms of Harrison Birtwistle and Michael Tippett. Its operatic culture was growing all the time and its concert-goers were inclined to accept modern works within a traditional menu, rather than form new music cliques and 'ghettos' as in Paris and Cologne. London was no longer a creative wasteland and did not need a dominant creed. It had acquired the courage to let a thousand flowers bloom, even when their colours clashed violently. The boundless variety of its musical life became the city's greatest cultural asset in modern times.

VISITING COMPOSERS AND WHERE THEY STAYED

BARTÓK, Béla   Aeolian Hall, Bond Street, W1
> At this under-used hall, owned by the BBC, Bartók made his mark with two recitals in 1924. He usually stayed in the South Kensington home (7 Sydney Place) of Duncan Wilson, His Majesty's Chief Inspector of Factories, and his wife, Freda, repaying their hospitality with piano lessons.

BELLINI, Vincenzo   Lived at 3 Old Burlington Street, W1, in 1833.

BERG, Alban   13 King Henry's Road, Hampstead, NW3
> At the home of Edward Clark, BBC producer and husband of the composer Elisabeth Lutyens, Berg passed a few nights in 1931 on his way to and from a composers' conference in Cambridge.

BERLIOZ, Hector   58 Queen Anne Street, W1
> His only surviving London residence. Berlioz lived here from 10 May to 28 July 1851, within easy reach of Hyde Park, where he was assessing instruments at the Great Exhibition. His other homes were at 27 Harley Street and 10 and 17 Old Cavendish Street.

BERNSTEIN, Leonard   Stayed at the Savoy Hotel.

BOULEZ, Pierre   Has a *pied-à-terre* in Kensington.

BRITTEN, Benjamin   Living mainly in Aldeburgh, Britten had sundry addresses in town but rarely stayed in London for long. Early on, he shared a flat with his sister at West Cottage Road, West End Green, West Hampstead, NW6, going to work in Soho Square with W. H. Auden in the GPO Film Unit. His triumphant *Peter Grimes* at Sadler's Wells on 7 June 1945 broke a new dawn in his music and London's. He founded his own publisher, Faber Music, at 3 Queen Square, WC1, and conducted at the opening of Queen Elizabeth Hall on 1 March 1967. On 7 May 1973 he underwent unsuccessful open-heart surgery at the National Heart Hospital, Westmoreland Street, W1.

Hector Berlioz.

BRUCKNER, Anton   Stayed at Seyd's, a German hotel (demolished), at 39 Finsbury Square in the City in 1871.

CHOPIN, Frédéric   4 St James's Place, SW1
Lived here mortally ill in October–November 1848 while preparing for the last concert of his life before returning to die in Paris. He had previously resided at 48 Dover Street, W1.

DEBUSSY, Claude-Achille   Hotel Cecil, The Strand, WC2
In 1902 and 1903 Debussy stayed at the hotel. On two subsequent visits he lived at 46 Grosvenor Street, W1, home of the German-born banker Edward Speyer; it is now the Japanese Embassy.

DVOŘÁK, Antonin   Stayed at 12 Hinde Street, Manchester Square, W1, the home of Oscar Beringer, who played the British première of his piano concerto; and with his publisher, Henry Littleton, at the palatial Westwood House (demolished), Crystal Palace. He often visited the National Gallery, exclaiming 'Mozart!' on seeing Raphael's Madonna.

ELGAR, Edward His longest London residence was Severn House (demolished), 42 Netherhall Gardens, Hampstead, NW3. After selling the house, he generally stayed at the Langham Hotel, W1.

FAURÉ, Gabriel 12 Bruton Street, W1
He stayed here in 1896 as a guest of Earl de Grey, with whom Puccini stayed in 1900. On other trips, Fauré was the guest of the artist John Singer Sargent at 31 Tite Street, SW3, and of Elgar's friend Frank Schuster at 22 Old Queen Street, SW1, overlooking St James's Park.

GERSHWIN, George His memories of 'A Foggy Day in London Town' stem from repeated visits. In 1924, the year of *Rhapsody in Blue*, he spent three months at 10 Berkeley Street, W1, working on a new show, *Primrose*, in which one number is entitled 'Berkeley Street and Kew'.

GOUNOD, Charles Tavistock House, Tavistock Square, Bloomsbury, WC1

Charles Gounod.

In a house formerly occupied by Charles Dickens, Gounod lived out a violent *ménage à trois* with Harry and Georgina Weldon, from 1871 to 1874.

GRAINGER, Percy   16 Cheyne Walk, Chelsea, SW3
The Australian composer surrendered his virginity here one night in 1902 to his patroness, Mrs Frank Lowry, who threatened to withdraw her money unless he mounted her. He thought he would die during orgasm.

HANDEL, George Frideric   25 Brook Street, W1
Handel bought his Mayfair house in 1723, wrote most of his masterpieces within it and died there on 14 April 1759. He had previously lived at Burlington House on Piccadilly, and with the Duke of Chandos at Edgware.

HAYDN, Joseph   18 Great Pulteney Street, W1, and 1 Bury Street, SW1 (both demolished)
On his first tour, Haydn took rooms with his impresario, Salomon. He was given a quiet corner in which to work in Broadwood's music shop across the road but found it hard to concentrate amid the city bustle and moved to spring quarters in the fields of Lisson Grove, NW8. On his return in 1794 he set up in Bury Street, near St James's Park and close to Rebecca Schroeter, a composer's widow with whom he had become intimate.

HESELTINE, Philip   12a Tite Street, Chelsea, SW3.
The pseudonymous composer Peter Warlock was born in the Savoy Hotel and died in a seedy apartment in Pimlico, waiting for a night when his mistress was away before putting out the cat and determinedly turning on the gas.

HENZE, Hans Werner   Has a coachman's house near Harrods, SW1.

HOLST, Gustav   St Paul's Girls School, Brook Green, W6
The Planets' composer earned his living as a teacher here, from 1905 to 1934, living nearby for some years at Barnes and writing locally inspired pieces like the *Brook Green Suite*. He also taught at Morley College.

IVES, Charles   Stayed at St James's Palace Hotel on five visits, from 1924 to 1938.

JANÁČEK, Leoš   Stayed at the Langham Hotel from 29 April to 8

May 1926. Located opposite the BBC, it was a favourite lodging for musicians.

LISZT, Franz   18 Great Marlborough Street, Oxford Circus, W1
Liszt made his London début in June 1824 when he was twelve years old, and lodged above the offices of the piano firm, Erard, close to the Argyll Concert Rooms.

MAHLER, Gustav   Stayed at Keyser's Royal Hotel, 69 Torrington Square, Bloomsbury, WC1 and at 22 Alfred Place, WC1, nearby (both demolished) on his only visit, when he conducted the 1892 *Ring* cycle at Covent Garden.

MENDELSSOHN, Felix   Hanover Square, W1
Mendelssohn's concert activities were centred around the famous concert rooms where, on 13 May 1833, he gave the world première of his Italian Symphony, with Bellini and Paganini in the audience. On ten trips to London he stayed mostly at 103 Great Portland Place, W1, and 4 Hobart Place, Victoria, SW1.

MOZART, Wolfgang Amadeus   19 Cecil Court, Leicester Square, WC2
The Mozarts stayed first above a barber's (now a music shop) in April 1764, then moved to 20 Thrift (now Frith) Street, Soho, W1 (at No. 22 next door, John Logie Baird gave the first demonstration of television in 1926). When Leopold fell ill, the family transferred to the cleaner air of Chelsea where, at 180 Ebury Street, SW1, the 8-year-old wrote his first symphony, telling his elder sister to remind him to include the horns.

PAGANINI, Niccolò   Stayed at a long-defunct hotel in Leicester Square, WC2.

PANUFNIK, Andrzej   Lived beside the river at Twickenham.

PHILIDOR, François-André Danican   Died at 10 Little Ryder Street (a demolished alley between King Street and Jermyn Street), SW1, on 31 August 1795. The funeral was held at St James's, Piccadilly, and he was buried behind St James's Chapel in Hampstead Road, NW1; the grave has been lost. His

Niccolò Paganini.

favourite chess club was Parsloe's, at 85 St James's Street, SW1.

PROKOFIEV, Sergei and PUCCINI, Giacomo   Preferred to stay at the Savoy Hotel.

PURCELL, Henry   Died in Marsham Street, Westminster, SW1.

RACHMANINOV, Sergei   Tended to stay at the Piccadilly Hotel (renamed Le Meridien), W1, on the site of the former St James's Hall.

RAVEL, Maurice   14 Holland Park, W11
Stayed with the singer Louise Alvar-Harding on visits between 1922 and 1932. In 1909 he lodged at 13 Cheyne Walk, Chelsea, SW3, with his pupil Vaughan Williams.

ROSSINI, Gioacchino   Stayed at 90 Regent Street, W1, on his only
    visit.

SAINT-SAËNS, Camille   Stayed at 49 George Street, W1, when he
    gave the world première of his Organ Symphony in May
    1886. Henry Wood was his host in 1902, at 4 Elsworthy Road,
    Hampstead, NW3.

SCHOENBERG, Arnold and WEBERN, Anton   Strand Palace
    Hotel, W1
    In January 1930 Schoenberg was accommodated by the BBC
    at this satisfactory hotel. Webern, invited six times by the
    BBC, also stayed here.

SIBELIUS, Jean   Stayed twice at the Langham Hotel.

STRAUSS, Richard   46 Grosvenor Street, W1
    Strauss was a guest of the music-loving financier Edward
    Speyer until the savings he invested with him were seques-
    trated as enemy property in 1914.

STRAVINSKY, Igor   Stayed at the Savoy, the Dorchester and the
    Ritz.

SULLIVAN, Arthur   Born at 8 Bolwell Street (demolished), Lam-
    beth, SE1.

SZYMANOWSKI, Karol   19 Edith Grove, SW3
    Stayed with his friends, the Drapers.

TCHAIKOVSKY, Pyotr Ilyich   Stayed in 1889 and 1893 at the
    Dieudonné Hotel (later the Eccentric Club) on Ryder Street,
    near St James's Hall, getting drunk alone in his room and cry-
    ing himself to sleep.

THOMSON, Virgil   Liked staying at the Travellers' Club, Pic-
    cadilly.

TIPPETT, Michael and NOVELLO, Ivor   HM Prison, Wormwood
    Scrubs, Acton, W3
    Tippett served a 3-month sentence in 1943 for failing to abide
    by the conditions of his exemption from military service; he

was visited by Britten. Novello did three weeks in 1942 for a motor offence.

VERDI, Giuseppe   Lived in 1862 on the site of Marylebone Station.

WAGNER, Richard   Lived at the King's Arms, Old Compton Street, Soho, W1, in 1839; at 22 Portland Terrace, Regent's Park in 1855; and at 12 Orme Square, Bayswater, W2, in 1877. None of his residences survives.

WEBER, Carl Maria von   Died of consumption at 91 Great Portland Street, W1.

WEILL, Kurt   Worked from January to July 1935 at Bramham Gardens, Earls Court, on a musical, *A Kingdom for a Cow*, that failed dismally. While living in the tiny flat he was reconciled with his ex-wife, Lotte Lenya, and emigrated with her to America.

4

REQUIEM FOR HALLOWED HALLS

Music in London has no home to call its own, no centrepoint of activity. The last decent concert hall was destroyed by German bombs on 10 May 1941, the night Hitler's deputy, Rudolf Hess, made his bizarre flight to Scotland. Since then, concerts have scattered in an ever-widening parabola around town and resources diffused in too many directions.

The forlorn photograph of Henry Wood standing among the twisted rubble of Queen's Hall conveys more than just the poignancy of an old man witnessing his life's work wiped out. It marked the end of an era when auditoria were architecturally imposing and acoustically ideal, and when the city had a focus for its musical activity. Wood went to his grave pleading for Queen's Hall to be reconstructed in replica on the same site.

Instead, London's new hall was raised on industrial wasteground on the wrong side of the river where no one would ever drop casually into a concert. Few people lived in the vicinity of Hungerford Bridge, and those who came to work nearby rushed to catch the commuter trains at Waterloo each night the moment five-thirty struck. The Royal Festival Hall offered scant refuge to weary office-workers. Constructed in stone, steel and concrete for the 1951 Festival of Britain, its exterior never fulfilled the designer's dream of a people's palace or justified its splendid vista, opposite the Houses of Parliament and within sight of St Paul's.

Inside, the 2,909 seats 'covered in lemon uncut moquette with a fine raised stripe' and separated by 'cream hide arms padded with foam rubber'[1] faded into a uniform brownish-grey, as dull as the hall's acoustics. It took several years of experiments before an acceptable sound was obtained, 168 microphones and speakers

Sir Henry Wood in the bombed ruins of Queen's Hall

being planted in the ceiling to give a discreet electronic boost to live orchestral music. Even so, the acoustics leave some liveliness to be desired.

The architects aimed to combine 'what is best in the German tradition ... with the English tradition founded more on the needs of choral singing'.[2] This indecisiveness, dictated by political considerations, resulted in a hall that provides an admirable sense of occasion with a lamentable shortage of reverberation. Choral and large-scale works feel compacted; a solo recitalist is virtually unseen from the hall's middle-distances. Like many ailing institutions, the Festival Hall was designated Royal and acquired a public, although few could love its faceless and fudged design.

Worse was to come. In 1967 the Queen Elizabeth Hall was added adjacently, blocking off what little majesty there was in the exterior of the larger hall, and turning the riverside promenade, already bleak, into a concrete maze of connecting walkways and dark alleys. The Purcell Room, Hayward Gallery and National Film Theatre took up what available space remained and beyond Westminster Bridge rose the National Theatre, latterly renamed

Royal. A stranger would find it impossible to identify these edifices as temples of art. Misplaced botches of mid-century functionalism, they look from the outside like nuclear reactors. The concrete has aged prematurely and is streaked with ineradicable grime. Beneath the walkways, adolescent youths test their skateboard speeds, drugs are traded and the homeless spend the nights in a pathetic cardboard city, an indictment and negation of the South Bank's cultural purpose. None of the world's great concert halls is so encased in human misery. To their credit, none of the South Bank's successive managements has tried to evict the trespassers, who have nowhere better to go. Responsibility for these conditions is legislated opposite at the Palace of Westminster, where ministers turn a blind eye to the outrage.

The concert halls were run until 1985, with varying degrees of inefficiency and squalor, by the London County Council and its successor, the Greater London Council. When the GLC was abolished by Margaret Thatcher for party-political reasons, the site was turned over to an unelected South Bank Board, funded by the Arts Council. A *laissez-faire* system of 'first come, first plays' was replaced with centralized planning which streamlined concerts into themes and series. While coordinated programming was generally applauded, the schemes imposed by the new directorate were arbitrary and sometimes disastrous. Seasons of Ligeti and Lutosławski, worthy enough on paper, played to halls that were two-thirds empty, damaging the South Bank finances and the credibility of the composers. A sequence of 'last works' by various composers had neither intellectual nor commercial validity. The strength of the South Bank lies not in what is performed but in who plays there, for the halls have always been a magnet to star performers.

A small library could be filled with plans to reorganize and redesign the troublesome South Bank, and the end is yet nowhere in sight. A proposal to knock down the walkways and erect an underground shopping mall perished with the 1990 recession. A rehearsal hall is desperately needed and there are rival claims for a dance studio, electronics laboratory, poetry library and parking space. Redevelopment remains in abeyance, and at the time of writing the South Bank continues to deteriorate physically.

Its centrist monopoly has been challenged and shattered by the Barbican Centre, built by the City of London at a cost of £153 million and opened in 1982 amid the self-congratulation that financiers turn on at the time of a takeover bid. Its theatre was destined for the Royal Shakespeare Company, space was provided for the Guildhall School of Music and Drama, and the heart of the complex was a 2,026-seat concert hall where the London Symphony Orchestra would establish residence. Acoustic tests revealed that it let in the noise of passing traffic and flushing toilets. The sound within the hall was not dispersed evenly, so that some seats were 'black spots' that could not pick up woodwind or cellos. Claudio Abbado, resident music director, demanded wood cladding to add warmth to the sonic ambience; but the deficiencies have not been fully treated and, ten years on and a million pounds later, miracle-working acousticians are still being called in to fire test-guns and propose improbable solutions. While Cardiff, Nottingham, Glasgow and Birmingham built state-of-the-art concert halls, London seemed fated to have singularly rotten acoustical luck with every hall that it constructed.

The disasters started with the Royal Albert Hall, erected in 1871 in memory of Victoria's late husband and possessing the interior acoustics of a municipal mausoleum. The hall was a swimming-pool of mushy notes that took a full 2.5 seconds to decay. At its inauguration ceremony, the Prince of Wales's speech was reported to have been 'heard in all parts of the building; in many parts it could be heard twice'.[3] A musical work receiving its first performance there, quipped Beecham, was immediately assured of a second.

In a bid to smother the notorious echo, the Albert Hall directors

The Royal Albert Hall in its early days.

took off its dome in 1949 and stuffed it with cotton wool. The suspension of plastic discs shaped like spacecraft ultimately soaked up excess reverberation and rendered the hall unrivalled for the outsized roar of Mahler's *Symphony of a Thousand* and Tchaikovsky's *1812 Overture*, complete with real cannon. For all its sepulchral aura, the Albert Hall possesses that inestimable 'atmosphere' that makes a great concert hall. It is, after all, one of the few places still standing where both Wagner and Verdi conducted their works.

At the time of its construction, London had the twin luxuries of Exeter Hall in the Strand, where Mendelssohn had played the organ and Berlioz conducted, and St James's Hall on Piccadilly, where Hans Richter stoutly performed Brahms while blacked-up Christy Minstrels plucked their banjos in the room below. St James's 'wasn't very comfortable and certainly not beautiful', recalled a conductor's daughter, yet 'I do not suppose that any concert hall has existed with more perfect acoustics'.[4] Once sanctuaries like these were consumed by fire or imperial developers' greed, orchestral activity concentrated for half a century in the much-adored Queen's Hall.

Opened in 1893 at the top of Regent Street, its centrality was cru-

St James's Hall in the 1870s.

cial to the development of concert-going habits and a coherent orchestral community. There were always other places in London to make music and meet music-lovers and many of them came free – whether as society soirées in which the greatest artists could be heard, or at philanthropic ventures like the South Place Concerts Society, where professional ensembles played to proletarian listeners. For £500 Fritz Kreisler would reappear after his nightly concert to entertain a ducal dinner, while rising stars like Pablo Casals and Arthur Rubinstein repaired post-recital to Muriel Draper's home at 31 Edith Grove, there to eat and play the night away. Young composers congregated around chamber venues like the Wigmore and Aeolian halls and supped in the cheap prototypes of Anthony Powell's novelized *Casanova's Chinese Restaurant*,[5] or among the bohemians in Regent Street's Café Royal. Each of the large clearing banks had an active orchestra of employees, and much interesting music was heard in the interludes at West End theatres.

Queen's Hall and its environs, however, were recognized by all classes and occupations as the epicentre of musical life. Its democratic character was established on opening night when the future King Edward VII queried the purpose of an ornate enclosure in the middle of the circle.

'That,' replied the directors, 'is the Royal Box, Sir.'

'You'll never see me in there,'[6] snorted Edward, ever a man of his word.

The box was removed and never restored, making Queen's Hall the only major theatre not to reserve space for the monarch. Where the royal posterior should have rested, youngsters in shorts and open-necked shirts, some wearing rucksacks, linked arms at the Proms.

'London is, of all great cities, the loneliest for young people,' noted the broadcaster C. E. M. Joad. 'There are no cafés in which to sit and talk hour after hour over the cup of coffee, and the young are too poor to afford clubs . . . The Proms came to serve as a sort of club.'[7] The stalls were surrounded with mirrors, and masks of the great composers beamed down on to the platform. Higher up, the seats were 'not very comfortable' but the social mix was broad. The novelist J. B. Priestley admired its 'bluey-green walls and gilded organ-pipes and lights shining through holes in the roof like fierce sunlight'.[8] The general colour scheme was a blend of terracotta and light grey, the precise shade of the belly of a London mouse, going by the witty architect's specifications. The ceiling, painted by a man from the Paris Opéra, was decorated with 'attenuated Cupids ... clad in sallow pantaloons'.[9] Performers considered it 'the most beloved concert hall in the world'.[10]

Outside the Proms season, high-priced concerts by international stars alternated with altruistic offerings from the Courtauld-Sargent Club, which offered subsidized tickets to office workers. Its initial series of six concerts in 1929 featured Artur Schnabel playing four concertos, Bruno Walter directing Mahler's unknown *Das Lied von der Erde* and Otto Klemperer making a stormy British début in the first UK performance of Bruckner's eighth symphony. On Saturdays, families packed the house for Robert Mayer's Children's Concerts. 'Meet you at Queen's Hall,' people said. It was a landmark in its own right.

When the bombs started falling in 1940, audiences stayed in their seats rather than seeking shelter, while orchestral players improvised until the all-clear sounded. 'Most astonishing,' remembered one stranded composer, 'was a complete performance of Mendelssohn's violin concerto, conducted and played by soloist and orchestra entirely from memory.'[11] After Wood retired to the wings one night, Adrian Boult led Haydn's Farewell Symphony in reverse, the players re-entering one by one. The climax of that particular air-raid was a Beecham imitation by one of the violinists that brought the house down and sent Boult out circulating with a wastepaper basket to collect contributions for the Musicians' Pensions Fund. The house was mercifully empty the night the

The exterior of Queen's Hall.

Luftwaffe struck on 10 May 1941, though the London Philharmonic lost almost all its instruments in the blaze.

The following afternoon, a Sunday, the public picked up their tickets from an improvised box-office beside the smoking ruins, drank a cup of tea at the orchestra's mobile canteen and walked up Portland Place to the re-scheduled concert, played on borrowed instruments, at the Royal Academy of Music. That day, the orchestra played 'like angels'.[12]

Flattened in the same attack was an institution of comparable importance to musicians. Pagani's restaurant on Great Portland Street was the after-concert venue where Sibelius once ate his way through the entire menu card in a single session and Caruso took a ripe peach into his astonishing gorge and swallowed it whole.[13] Pagani's was an indispensable adjunct to Queen's Hall. Wood planned his first Prom on one of its tablecloths, the LSO held crisis board meetings there, and the London Philharmonic saw off Beecham at a lavish farewell dinner. John Barbirolli, born nearby, held his wedding reception upstairs.

The neighbouring pub was an unofficial employment exchange for musicians. The George at 55 Great Portland Street, known as 'the Gluepot' because orchestral members would get stuck there in the interval, employed a man with a handbell to summon them back to duty. With the BBC around the corner in Langham Place, players elbowed their way to the bar through a bevy of hard-drinking stars, among them the poets Dylan Thomas and Louis MacNeice, and the composers William Walton and Constant Lambert, known to players as 'Connie' and revered for his awesome intellect, when sober. The George withstood the war but lost its nickname and loyal clientèle with the disappearance of Queen's Hall.

The bustling streets behind Oxford Circus were home to a community of musicians bound by ties of blood and business. Of the dynasties that flourished around Queen's Hall, the Goossens brood was the most prolific, two sons of a Liverpool-Belgian conductor who came to study in London, Eugene joining Henry Wood's first violins, Léon playing oboe in Arthur Nikisch's LSO. Eugene Goossens became a composer and international conductor; Léon was the supreme oboist, star of Toscanini and Beecham recordings and venerated teacher for most of the century. Their younger sisters, Sidonie and Marie, both played harp in the London orchestras well into their eighties. At a memorable family Prom given in 1958, Léon and the ladies played Eugene's Concert

Piece for two harps and oboe.

The Brains blazed away in the horn section. Aubrey Brain played for Beecham and the BBC, his brother Alfred served Henry Wood before winding up as principal of the Los Angeles Philharmonic. Dennis Brain, Aubrey's son, was a phenomenon, the outstanding French-horn player in Europe and dazzling inspiration of Britten's *Serenade for Tenor, Horn and Strings* and Paul Hindemith's Concerto. His death in a car-smash at the age of thirty-six was a shattering loss. Yet, at the next Philharmonia concert, Alan Civil moved up one seat and assumed his mantle, testifying to the depth of home-grown talent and versatility in London's orchestras. Civil later played solo on the Beatles' track, 'For No One'.

The intimacy of their professional and family lives bred a powerful ethos and solidarity among orchestral players. It also bred successive generations who regarded orchestral work as their ancestral craft. Sons and daughters followed their parents into the ranks – not by means of string-pulling, but by proving themselves proficient in blind auditions. The sons of Archie Camden, bassoonist of the BBC and RPO, were typical products of this society. Kerry, the elder, blew his father's instrument in various ensembles; Anthony became principal oboe in the LSO and its chairman for twelve turbulent years.

Carl Pini, sometime leader of the Philharmonia, was the son of Anthony Pini, Beecham's principal cellist at the London Philharmonic. Neville Marriner, who played violin in the LSO, has a son, Andrew, who is now their principal clarinet. The same orchestra premièred Oliver Knussen's first symphony when he was just fifteen; his proud father, Stuart Knussen, was a member of the double-basses.

Members of the London orchestras held themselves apart from other musical sectors. Despite moonlighting and occasional migrations to opera and ballet, they kept their own company and married their own sort. There is little of the backstage intimacy – let alone marriage – between players and singers that prospers in European opera houses. The operatic values of star singers and dictatorial directors contradict the egalitarian ideals of these fiercely autonomous musicians, who look pityingly upon the pit-players as servile wage-slaves.

In their view – and it is not an isolated one – opera, for all its eye-catching extravagance, is merely the icing on London's musical cake. Its history wavers between divas and financial disasters, with the brief golden ages of Malibran and Patti, Melba and Sutherland, mingled with grey decades of dashed hopes and insolvency. Its public was traditionally wealthy and élitist, suppering at the Savoy, where chef Escoffier named his peach dessert after Dame Nellie. State subsidy created a broader and more knowledgeable audience, but seat prices are far too high for middle-class couples to afford as a weekly (or even monthly) treat, and opera remains a luxury that most Londoners learn to live without, except on record or on television.

Orchestral music, on the other hand, is their daily bread. Costing less than the price of a compact disc, it is readily accessible, richly varied and robustly performed. 'For anyone bored with successive Karajan recordings of the same classical masterpiece, the London scene offers some enlightening alternatives,'[14] suggests one recent review. Ingrained rivalry between the orchestras ensures a continuous creative tension and competitive edge that has resisted tidy 'rationalization' plans and merger proposals. The effervescence within the orchestras is palpable. While well-paid jobs stand vacant for months in State-run German orchestras, every London opening is vigorously contested.

Each orchestra has a core of supporters, loyal as football fans, who tag along to fixtures at Salzburg and Carnegie Hall and cheer their lads to the echo. Backstage after any concert, home or away, players mingle glass in hand with friends, loved-ones and potential loved-ones in a conviviality tinged with relief and mutual self-admiration. The green rooms of London are invariably thronged, but players love to be greeted on tour by acquaintances old and new.

The personality of each London orchestra is separate and distinct, an amalgam of the spirit of its players past and present. Conductors come and go without touching its collective identity. The Berlin Philharmonic was Karajan's band; the LSO was never anything but itself – the rebellious enterprise of four brass players in a steam train still percolates the company. This oldest of London orchestras is also the rowdiest and most sentimental. Disenchanted with a domineering Viennese conductor, Josef Krips, it sent him packing with a punch in the teeth. Devastated when one of its members falls seriously ill, the others discreetly support his family out of their own pockets. The LSO periodically rises against conductors and managers and never bothers to hide its laundry from the press. Behind the brashness is a whole-hearted dedication to playing that attracts conductors as diverse as Pierre Boulez and Leonard Bernstein, Claudio Abbado and André Previn.

The London Philharmonic are a rather more level-headed lot.

THE ROYAL PHILHARMONIC
1937   SOCIETY   1938

SERIES A	SERIES B
Thursday, October 14th	**Thursday, October 28th**
BEECHAM — Mass in D .. .. *Beethoven*; "Dettingen" Te Deum .. .. *Handel* LEEDS FESTIVAL CHORUS ISOBEL BAILLIE MARY JARRED HEDDLE NASH HAROLD WILLIAMS	**BEECHAM** — Overture: "La Scala di Seta" .. *Rossini*; Violoncello Concerto .. .. *Boccherini*; "Antar" .. .. *Rimsky-Korsakov*; Hebrew Rhapsody, "Schelomo" *Ernest Bloch*; "Romeo and Juliet" .. .. *Tchaikovsky* PIATIGORSKY
Thursday, November 4th	**Thursday, November 18th**
BOULANGER — Selection from "Dardanus" .. .. *Rameau*; Sonata sopra Sancta Maria, Lamento della Ninfa, "Lasciatemi morire" .. *Monteverdi*; Concerto for Harpsichord .. .. *Haydn*; Requiem Mass .. .. *Fauré* LUCILLE WALLACE GISÈLE PEYRON M. B. de POLIGNAC I. KEDROFF P. DERENNE HUGUES CUÉNOD DODA CONRAD THE ORIANA CHOIR & A CAPPELLA SINGERS (Conductor: C. Kennedy Scott)	**BEECHAM** — Symphony in B flat, No. 102 .. *Haydn*; Introduction and Allegro for Strings .. *Elgar*; Dance Rhapsody No. 1 .. .. *Delius*; Symphony in A minor, Op. 44 .. *Rachmaninoff* (First Performance in Europe)
Thursday, December 2nd	**Thursday, January 13th**
BEECHAM — Symphony No. 6, Symphony No. 7, Symphony No. 4, Suite: "Karelia" .. .. } *Sibelius*	**HEWARD** — Overture: "Ivan the Terrible" *Rimsky-Korsakov*; "Winter—Spring" .. .. *Ernest Bloch*; Pianoforte Concerto in D minor .. *Brahms*; Symphony in G minor .. *E. J. Moeran* (First Performance) MYRA HESS
Thursday, January 27th	**Thursday, February 10th**
MENGELBERG — Sinfonia .. .. *Johann Christian Bach*; Three movements from "Psyché" *César Franck*; Prelude and Liebestod ("Tristan") .. *Wagner*; Symphony No. 5 in E minor .. *Tchaikovsky*	**WEINGARTNER** — Symphony in G ("Military") .. *Haydn*; Symphony in G minor .. .. *Mozart*; Symphony No. 2 in D .. .. *Beethoven*
Thursday, February 24th	**Thursday, March 10th**
WEINGARTNER — "Der Freischütz" Overture .. *Weber*; Symphony No. 3 in F .. .. *Brahms*; Symphony No. 7 in C .. .. *Schubert*	**BEECHAM** — Symphony in E flat .. .. *Mozart*; Pianoforte Concerto in G. K.453 .. *Mozart*; Symphony in D .. .. *Boccherini* (First London Performance) "Haffner" Symphony .. .. *Mozart* LOUIS KENTNER
Thursday, March 24th	**Thursday, April 7th**
BEECHAM — Overture: "Die Meistersinger" .. *Wagner*; Suite for Viola .. *Vaughan Williams*; "L'Après-midi d'un Faune" .. *Debussy*; Double Concerto .. .. *Arthur Benjamin* (First Performance) Symphony No. 1 in B flat .. .. *Schumann* EDA KERSEY BERNARD SHORE	**BEECHAM** — Overture: "A Midsummer Night's Dream" .. .. .. *Mendelssohn*; Pianoforte Concerto .. .. *John Ireland*; Ballet Music: "Checkmate" .. *Arthur Bliss* (First Concert Performance) "Ein Heldenleben" .. .. .. *Strauss* CLIFFORD CURZON

THE LONDON PHILHARMONIC ORCHESTRA

Adventurous fare for the late 1930s: three premières, a woman conductor and the first London performance of Fauré's Requiem.

68

Abandoned by Beecham, they chose conductors with caution: the safety-first Dutchmen Eduard van Beinum and Bernard Haitink, the solid English virtues of Adrian Boult. The orchestra then fell into a passionate relationship with the hyper-tense Mahlerian Klaus Tennstedt, who was plagued by natural disaster and obliged to give way to a steely-eyed, 30-year-old Austrian prodigy, Franz Welser-Möst. London Philharmonic musicians tend to be hard-working craftsmen, uninterested in commercial matters or after-hours conviviality, but prepared to play with a leg in plaster and a wife in labour if needed for a concert. Their strength lies in the late romantic repertoire and a star-studded woodwind section. In the corporate fever of the 1980s, players surrendered their anarchic autonomy and vested control in an executive board comprised partly of city businessmen and politicians.

The Philharmonia retains something of the swagger of its 1950s' heyday despite artistic and financial attrition. It has hitched its fortunes in the 1990s to the debatable interpretations of the Italian conductor, Giuseppe Sinopoli, and has reaped the benefits of his record contract and enormous popularity in Japan. It has also won an unlikely annual residence at the Châtelet Theatre in Paris, testimony to the high esteem for London musicianship in continental Europe, a reputation secured by a half-century of excellent recordings.

The Royal Philharmonic, Beecham's last creation, flourished in the 1980s' gold-rush but blotted its copybook with unadventurous programming and an inexplicable knack of appearing in two cities on the same night, a tendency that provoked public scandal and legal action. The RPO suffered a punitive cut in its Arts Council grant in 1992 and seems to be in a process of reconstruction under its shyly intense music director, Vladimir Ashkenazy.

The fifth of London's full-strength orchestras, the BBC Symphony, is the only one in which players earn a steady wage. Its future and theirs are, however, jeopardized by the disintegration of a State broadcasting system starved of political support and sufficient funding. Three BBC regional orchestras went to the wall in 1980 despite a national strike by musicians, and threats of incipient privatization now hang above the flagship ensemble. The orchestra has struggled to define a clear-cut identity since the heady days of Boulez's revolution when it camped at the foreground of avant-gardism. It continues to be generously well-rehearsed and equal to the most abstruse modern scores, but its public concerts are poorly attended and only the annual Proms provide economic justification for its continued existence. Since the BBC seems intent on sub-leasing the Proms to outside contractors, the symphony orchestra survives on its frayed nerves. Its present conductor is the boyishly enthusiastic Andrew Davis.

In addition to the big five, four full-time chamber orchestras of varying size ply their wares in the city. The Academy of St Martin-in-the-Fields was formed by Neville Marriner from disgruntled fellow-members of the LSO and became the most recorded ensemble in the world. The English Chamber Orchestra enjoyed a formative connection with Benjamin Britten. The London Mozart Players spanned classical and neo-classical repertoires and made its base at Croydon. And the London Sinfonietta is a new music ensemble which has given almost 200 world premières. Players often alternate between the chamber and symphony orchestras, but a clear demarcation exists between the ensembles in each sector.

Any change in the status of one of the orchestras would have drastic and unforeseeable consequences for the rest, the more so since their traditional economy has been undermined in the past decade with most film-track and advertising work migrating to Munich and Budapest. Despite session fees abroad of £16 a head, one-quarter of the London rate, some producers were prepared to pay over the odds for the versatility of London players, until recessionary pressures virtually killed off the sector. For the first time since 1929 there were too many musicians in London chasing too few jobs.

Those orchestras which look likeliest to weather the storm are the ones that took steps to safeguard their artistic priorities when the going was good. The LSO and the London Philharmonic began rationalizing their schedules some years before the crisis, alarmed at the human and musical toll of a working week that could exceed seventy hours for principal players. Several outstanding musicians had opted for a poorer existence in provincial orchestras in a move to save their health and their marriages. To stem the drain of talent, both orchestras hired two principals to share the work in each section. In addition to easing the workload, this gave the players more time in their private lives to teach, rehearse and pursue solo careers. It made for happier orchestras, and wealthier ones, as the Arts Council endorsed the initiative with million-pound annual grants. Implicitly it also set two of the orchestras apart from the others as the premier standard-bearers of London music.

This split into two leagues was reinforced by the residencies won by the LSO at the Barbican in 1982 and by the London Philharmonic at the South Bank from 1992, a security of tenure that gave them both psychological and commercial advantages. Knowing that they have first choice of dates for the rest of the century enables the orchestras to plan ambitious seasons, book the best soloists and secure long-term financial commitments. The move to the Barbican almost ruined the LSO, which experimented with esoteric composers and repeat-concerts without testing the market beforehand. It survived a gruelling couple of years, when players paid £43 a week into a rescue fund and worked every hour of the clock, slowly building a faithful audience that was prepared to follow where the orchestra led. While the Royal Shakespeare Company had to close its Barbican theatre for months to cut its deficit, the LSO was playing cycles of Shostakovich and Schnittke to full and appreciative houses. It learned the lessons of residency the hard way and yet, paradoxically, needs the London Philharmonic to establish a challenging concurrence at the South Bank in order to confirm its own success.

More by error than by planning, London has found itself on the brink of an exciting musical era, with two orchestras that have the artistic and commercial confidence to dictate a credible and coherent season. The London Philharmonic's path to residency was paved with intrigue and misfortune. Promised primacy back in 1951, it was pushed out by Conservative councillors who were told that its manager, Thomas Russell, was a dangerous communist who spent his holidays in China. A joint-residency initiative with the Philharmonia was shelved by the Arts Council, and the Philharmonia itself furiously rejected a merger proposal from the London Philharmonic, an apparent takeover bid that left a legacy of bad blood. When an independent inquiry ruled that the London Philharmonic was best equipped to make a success of residency, the Philharmonia was left struggling to retain its foothold on the South Bank.

Like the Royal Philharmonic, it has taken to the road, touring to all parts of the world on the strength of its recorded reputation and aiming to build a following in both suburban and provincial halls. Nevertheless, both orchestras need to present a strong central London season as the basis of their *raison d'être*.

Even for the orchestras in residence, life remains a frantic shuttle through traffic jams and fug from one draughty rehearsal room to the next recording studio. Players are forever flitting from

Watford in the north to Woolwich in the south-east to prepare for a concert they will play at the South Bank. A church in Southwark, converted into a rehearsal hall and sentimentally re-christened Henry Wood Hall, is hopelessly overbooked. Recordings are centred on Abbey Road but overflow to empty churches and, for choral extravaganzas, to the so-called three Ws – the town halls at Walthamstow, Watford and Wembley. Commuting is the bane of every orchestral player's existence.

As they career around town and across the world, the delicate fabric of musical society has begun to disentangle. There is no Pagani's restaurant where they eat and marry, no George pub where they meet for a drink. The Festival Hall and Barbican have none of the homeliness of Queen's Hall, and neither is blessed with congenial hostelries. At the South Bank, in particular, there is not enough room for musicians to store their belongings, and backstage thefts are so endemic that players carry all their valuables out on to the concert platform. Unless the two centres can radiate a sense of belonging, musicians will feel alienated and lose the communality that gave music in London its singular strength. In any opinion poll of players, few – if any – will voice affection for their present concert halls.

One hall alone still elicits unqualified warmth from its artists and patrons. The Wigmore Hall, within earshot of old Queen's Hall, is a blowsy late-romantic salon with 700-odd seats. Installed by a German piano manufacturer to advertise his wares, it was seized by the public authorities in 1914 as enemy property and managed by them ever since. Its monthly programme alternated débutants with world stars like Arthur Rubinstein and Elena Gerhardt, who would return year after year in sentimental remembrance of their triumphant début. The intimacy within is matched by the interval informality when concert-goers in every kind of dress mingle on the deserted pavement or form lifelong relationships in the ice-cream crush. The acoustics are natural and the atmosphere intense. Visitors can readily imagine the wartime fervour of Peter Pears and Dennis Brain giving the first performance of Benjamin Britten's *Serenade for Tenor, Horn and Strings,* or Michael Tippett arriving straight from prison that year to hear a performance of his second string quartet. The Wigmore is the last vestige of the heartland of London's music. It stands as a memorial and a warning to the waning communality of professional musicians.

5

AN EXOTICK AND
IRRATIONAL
ENTERTAINMENT

In an orchestral citadel, opera takes a back seat. Berlin, which bran-
dishes its Philharmonic as a cultural icon, has made little capital of
its opera houses. In Leipzig, the State opera lives in the shadow of
the illustrious Gewandhaus. Amsterdam was made an opera-free
zone under Willem Mengelberg, anxious to protect his Concert-
gebouworkest. By way of retaliation, no orchestra of any consequence has survived in the homeland of Italian opera. Evidently,
the musical sisters cannot co-exist in peaceable equality.

In London, ringed defensively by orchestras, the growth of
opera was further stunted by two infernal factors – class warfare
and xenophobia. Opera was traditionally for toffs, staged during
the London Season to amuse the landed gentry, who spent the
early summer months in town raiding the big stores and parading
their marriageable daughters. Poorer folk crowded the upper galleries, and mercantile impresarios bore the brunt of the risk, but
there was never any question which class called the tune at the
opera – a class that continues to hold sway in these supposedly
classless times. In modern State-funded companies, the aristocracy has been augmented on the board by bankers, media mag-
nates and supermarket owners. The interests represented at the
governing level of British opera remain those of a social élite.

As if this fiscal exclusivity were not enough to limit the popular
base of opera, the art was received from its inception as a foreign
implant, devised by immoral and illogical continentals. 'There is
nothing that has more startled our English Audience,' wrote the
columnist Joseph Addison on seeing Handel's *Rinaldo* in 1711,
'than the Italian Recitativo at its first Entrance upon the Stage.
People were wonderfully surprised to hear Generals singing the

73

A ticket designed by Hogarth.

Word of Command and Ladies delivering Messages in Musick. Our Countrymen could not forbear laughing ...'[1] Addison, who spoke a few words of Italian, attacked the florid texts with their 'tedious circumlocutions, as are used by none but peasants in our own country'.[2] Otiose phrases and musical ululation, he argued, held up the drama, which was, in any case, murky or meaningless.

Those who succumbed to the spell of Italian opera tended to ignore the plot altogether. 'Whenever I go to an opera, I leave my sense and reason at the door with my half guinea, and deliver myself up to my eyes and my ears,'[3] averred the politician, Lord Chesterfield. Tone-deaf Dictionary Johnson defined opera as 'an exotick and irrational entertainment', a sentiment echoed two centuries later by the poet Auden, who declared that 'no good opera plot can be sensible, for people do not sing when they are feeling sensible'.[4]

The deeper prejudice, though, was insular. Opera was an alien product which, in its Italian and French incarnations, reeked of Catholic mores and Mediterranean character, while in its German guise it looked as dark as the Schwarzwald and as heavy as a chocolate torte. The Englishman liked his music either light and plain, or solemnly sacrosanct. Opera offended both tastes.

English composers applied themselves to oratorios of the highest purity, abhorring the operatic aberration. Elgar never wrote an opera (though he once toyed with a Thomas Hardy theme) and Walford Davies used his weekly slot on the BBC to decry the art in all its corruptive vulgarity. 'I hold a presumptuous belief that Opera and Wagner has damaged our wits,' he pontificated, 'that they have had a temporarily vicious influence on the highest abstract forms.'[5] Delius, Holst and Vaughan Williams dabbled unsuccessfully in musical dramas. Dame Ethel Smyth, a Valkyrie by appearance, recruited her royal connections to attend her premières, only to hear Edward VII threaten to get up and leave the next time that damned noise woke him again.

Gilbert ...

It was left to Irishmen, ever the outsiders in London's demography, to supply a local alternative to the Italian and German output at Covent Garden. The most celebrated was Arthur Sullivan, who spiced up W. S. Gilbert's acerbic scripts, mocked the entire genre by satirizing bel canto arias in *Trial by Jury* and parodied Isolde's theme in *Iolanthe*.

Her Majesty was not amused and, in between comic operas, Sullivan was urged to atone for his levity with rousing hymns and religious anthems, among them 'Onward Christian soldiers'. Victoria implored him to write something serious for the stage, but Sullivan's best shot, *Ivanhoe*, turned out to be a poor pastiche of Verdi and Wagner.

For most of the nineteenth century the banner of British opera was borne by the Irishman Michael Balfe, a baritone duettist with

. . and Sullivan – melancholy figures of fun.

Maria Malibran. His folkish music drama *The Bohemian Girl* (1843) was translated into Italian, French and German and played in every capital of Europe and the Americas. It ran longer in London than any show since *The Beggar's Opera* and held its appeal until the end of the century as the centrepiece of a notional 'English *Ring'*, alongside *Maritana* (1845) by Vincent Wallace of Waterford and Julius Benedict's *Lily of Killarney* (1862). Then it mysteriously evanesced into the mists of time. A 1951 Covent Garden revival conducted by Beecham was yawned off the boards, laid bare in its irretrievable triviality.

With the prospect of an English opera *sui generis* seeming unlikely, a strident clique of idealists sought other means of operatic liberation. They determined to demystify and democratize the alien art by rendering it in the Queen's own English – to create an opera sung in the vernacular yet equal in performance to the best that Milan and Vienna could provide. Made comprehensible and affordable, opera would at last appeal to the sensation-seeking masses, pay its way at the box-office and strike roots in the bedrock of British creativity.

Many were the proselytes who pursued this holy grail, and many were the fortunes and lives that it consumed. An early martyr was Carl Rosa, a Hamburg fiddler with a diva wife who, in 1875, packed out the Princess' Theatre in Oxford Street with an English-sung *Figaro*. 'This London public is now ripe for English opera of a better sort,' he proclaimed. 'It longs for something more than ballad-operas and a "star" or two. It wants good works and, above all, a good ensemble.'[6]

Rosa formed a touring company and, for five limelight years, jointly ran the Drury Lane Theatre with Augustus Harris, producing Anglicized Verdi, early Wagner and some English ephemeralities until the stress and excitement of it all killed him at the vulnerable age of forty-seven. His profits amounted to a substantial £78,000, enabling the Carl Rosa company to carry on touring opera in English up and down the land, sometimes in two or three towns on the same night, until it merged in 1958 with Sadler's Wells. It gave the first British performances of Massenet's *Manon* and Puccini's *La Bohème* and, although unnoticed abroad, several of its singers attained celebrity, the most notable being Eva Turner, who stormed La Scala as the archetype Turandot.

Rosa's partner took the opposite route to an identical fate. The enterprising son of a Covent Garden stage manager, Augustus Harris was unimpressed with comprehensible opera and, having

Carl Rosa company production of Cavalleria Rusticana *with Eva Turner as Santuzza.*

presented London's first *Tristan* at Drury Lane, took over Covent Garden to inaugurate its finest era. Alongside the everlasting Adelina Patti, who starred for twenty-five consecutive seasons, he introduced the Australian Nellie Melba, who lasted even longer, and soon all the world's great singers flocked to a house that he revitalized with fresh investment and the inevitable blue-blood involvement. He imported Verdi's original *Otello* protagonists, Tamagno and Maurel; the brothers de Reszke; the amazing Lilli Lehmann of 165 roles; Emma Eames, Albani, Calvé, Schumann-Heink, Sembrich, Ternina – voices that crackle from the earliest gramophone cylinders, many of them recorded in London. Covent Garden changed its name from the Royal Italian Opera when he imported its first *Ring*, lock, stock and orchestra from Hamburg, along with an abrasive young conductor, Gustav Mahler.

Harris took control of the Rosa company when its founder died, bought the *Sunday Times* to appease its music critic, and engaged Major Horatio Herbert Kitchener to drill the soldiers' chorus in *Faust*. He expired suddenly in the summer of 1896, at forty-four years of age, having drawn world attention to a London opera house for the first time in half a century.

His triumph failed to extinguish the virtue of indigenous

Augustus Harris of Drury Lane.

opera and its partisans. On the contrary, it encouraged them to seek parity as an alternative, but equal, art form. Charles Villiers Stanford, the ebullient Dublin-born composer of seven picturesque symphonies and seven largely picaresque operas, took up the cudgels with a public petition to the London County Council for the erection of a national opera house on the north bank of the Thames. It would cost £100,000 to build and would need £10,000 a year in subsidy. The town of Geneva, wrote Stanford witheringly, had built an opera house for £152,000 and granted it £7,500 a year. Surely London deserved no less, and could afford rather more?

Not so, in the view of the municipal authorities who, after 'careful consideration', shelved the proposal and proceeded to spend £300,000 on a Thames steamboat shuttle. Music was not a priority for politicians, who were elected to keep the buses running and the drains clear. Nor did Stanford's imperial desire 'to make clear our position in the world and to assure its permanence'[7] cut much ice with Westminster. In 1908, the House of Commons voted to spend £341,731 on museums, art and literature and a measly £1,000 on music – to be shared equally between the Royal Academy and the Royal College. 'The most difficult rock to surmount is prejudice, the fixed, innate dislike of Englishmen to make a new departure,'[8] grumbled the disconsolate composer.

Deprived of a home, the Anglicists stormed the polyglot portals of Covent Garden with a *Ring* sung in English under the baton of its first Bayreuth conductor, Hans Richter. It had the blessing of Cosima Wagner, and Richter believed himself to be laying 'the foundation of permanent English opera'. In a statement to the press, he added, 'If this goal is reached, or at least the way prepared for it, I shall have achieved one of my highest aims and embodied my gratitude for the hospitality which has been unstintedly and unceasingly bestowed on me in this country for thirty years.'[9] The *Ring*, replete with local talent, was a resounding success for two seasons in 1908 and 1909, but Richter's ambitions were thwarted by the noble dilettantes who ran Covent Garden as a vehicle for glamorous stars and popular repertoire.

'It is not a question of language at all,' insisted the chairman of the Grand Opera Syndicate, Harry V. Higgins. 'The fact is, that unless for some very special attraction, the London public will not come to the opera in sufficient numbers to make it pay ... There is very little demand for Opera at all outside the season; and outside a small circle of those who have an axe of their own to grind, the idea that a craving exists for opera to be given in

J. Lapuchin

THE LEGEND OF THE INVISIBLE CITY

OF

KITESH

AND

THE MAIDEN FEVRONIA

LIBRETTO BY · · W. I. BIELSKY

MUSIC BY

N. RIMSKY-KORSAKOV

A CONCERT VERSION. GIVEN FOR THE FIRST TIME IN ENGLAND

AT THE

ROYAL OPERA HOUSE, COVENT GARDEN

MARCH THIRTIETH, 1926

THE BRITISH BROADCASTING CO. L^TD.

English is an absolute delusion.'[10]

Afflicted by an acute form of that delusion was a rich young Lancastrian who trumped the *Ring* in 1910 with a burst of entertainments with which he meant to convince the English once and for all of the necessity of opera. Over the next half-century, Thomas Beecham would spend his father's pharmaceutical fortune, his mistress's dowry and any other income he could appropriate on the profitless and usually thankless task of producing opera. He opened with a year-long season of 190 performances, whose electrifying high point was the local première of *Elektra*. Richard Strauss and Bruno Walter joined him as co-conductors and the public response was so rewarding that Oscar Hammerstein founded a rival London company.

For five years until the outbreak of war, Beecham enthralled London with a succession of near-scandals that included a scantily clad *Salome* and Diaghilev's Ballets Russes in the second production of Stravinsky's *Rite of Spring*, six weeks after it provoked Parisian riots. Flitting from Covent Garden to Drury Lane when the syndicate gave him trouble, Beecham manipulated the social connections of his American-born paramour, Lady Cunard, to acquire a fashionable cachet. Many of his productions were rough and ready and several sank for want of dramatic input, among them Delius's *Village Romeo and Juliet*. Beecham grumbled that the English had no interest in novelty and that any time he tried out an unknown opera they fled as if from the plague. He persisted regardless, exploring byways of Russian and French opera, and demonstrating an unwavering commitment to a handful of English composers: Ethel Smyth, who bankrolled her own operas; Joseph Holbrooke, who enjoyed a vogue as a bombastic modernist; and Frederick Delius, to whom he was eternally devoted and whose music he performed with unequalled conviction and lucidity.

Beecham's stance on the contentious issue of vernacular opera was, however, inconsistent. While at Covent Garden, he espoused original languages and declared the idea of a national opera house to be 'preposterous, futile and idiotic'.[11] During the war – with xenophobia so rampant that a dachshund was kicked to death in Berkhamsted for being of German breed – he recanted and formed the Beecham Opera Company to promote opera in English at the Shaftesbury and Aldwych theatres, with additional runs in Manchester. Using sets left behind by Diaghilev and the best singers he could find, Beecham once again set the art alight, until the death of his father forced his company into liquidation and its conductor into the bankruptcy courts.

From the wreckage there emerged a British National Opera Company whose aims were writ large in its title. 'We have not only to build up a large repertoire of foreign operas in English,' urged the conductor Albert Coates, a refugee from the Russian revolution, 'but an English national opera, to be perfect, must have an English national repertoire, works written by English poets with music composed by English musicians.'[12] BNOC sparked a minor creative revival and staged premières by Holst and Vaughan Williams. But the London public was unimpressed and the company suffered heavy losses in the capital before collapsing in 1928. Beecham, chafing at his exclusion, called it 'a company of vagrants inhabiting spiritual lodging-houses'.[13] He put together on paper an Imperial League of Opera, 'the largest organization of its kind in the world',[14] before losing interest in the English language and returning to star-struck international opera at Covent Garden.

The grail of opera in English passed to Sadler's Wells in the grimy north of London, where a sometime violinist, Lilian Baylis, persuaded the borough council of Islington to repair the derelict house and fund her opera and ballet companies. Public appeals and individual donations made up the rest. The singing was adequate rather than spectacular, but in Sadler's Wells an ethos was formed that would bring about the long-awaited rebirth of British opera.

On 7 June 1945, one month after Germany surrendered, Sadler's Wells reopened in a bombed-out neighbourhood with an opera which, within three years, would be produced in Stockholm, Zurich, Basle, Antwerp, Tanglewood, Hamburg, Berlin and Budapest; at La Scala, Milan, the Metropolitan Opera and at Covent Garden itself. No new opera had so swept the world's boards since Puccini died; and Benjamin Britten's *Peter Grimes* was anything but a tuneful crowd-pleaser. The harrowing account of a Suffolk fisherman accused of mistreating small boys was set to salty music of a dark and riveting complexity.

Grimes was nurtured in the crucible of Sadler's Wells, which Britten's partner in life, the tenor Peter Pears, joined in 1943 after their return from America. He brought the composer to performances and introduced him to the inner circle, which comprised the administrator, Tyrone Guthrie, chief conductor Lawrance Collingwood and principal soprano, Joan Cross. Britten's presence, though, was unwelcome to others in the company. They objected to his pacifism and homosexuality and rejected the storm-swept opera as 'a piece of cacophony'.[15] The key role of Balstrode had to be recast during rehearsals and, in the première week, a coterie of leading singers attempted to overthrow the management in a protest against the opera and its composer.

It was an unsettling début for the 31-year-old Britten, who

Benjamin Britten after the Peter Grimes *triumph.*

credited Sadler's Wells with having 'considerably influenced both the shape and the characterization of the opera'.[16] Many in the first-night audience recognized not only the emergence of an important new voice, but 'perhaps also the dawn of a new period when English opera would flourish in its own right'.[17] Towards the end of his life Britten reflected, 'I think it broke the ice for British opera.'[18]

His opponents, however, quickly gained the upper hand and *Grimes* was taken off after seven performances, despite playing to full houses and prompting the conductor on the no. 19 bus to announce outside Sadler's Wells, 'This way for Peter Grimes, the sadistic fisherman.'[19] Its removal split the company and Britten, Pears, Cross and the producer Eric Crozier broke away to form an

English Opera Group, 'dedicated to the creation of new works, performed with the least possible expense and capable of attracting new audiences'.[20] The chance for a London opera house to work with a major composer in residence was sacrificed on an altar of petty prejudices. Britten's next opera, *The Rape of Lucretia*, was written for Glyndebourne and Edinburgh.

At the peak of its prominence – and while applying to take over the moribund Covent Garden theatre, which had been operating in wartime as a dance-hall – Sadler's Wells Opera proved itself incapable of playing the central role. It was Covent Garden that seized the moment, stealing the opposition's policies to declare its intention henceforth of presenting opera in English. British singers need never again play makeweights to imported world stars. On the contrary, luminaries like Hans Hotter, Kirsten Flagstad and Ljuba Welitsch who came to Covent Garden would be required to relearn their roles in English; and most did so willingly, for work was scarce on the continent of Europe.

There were loud objections to this change of policy, not all of them unreasonable. Opera in translation contorted its clauses into impossible knots to keep pace with the music. 'The traitor my honour who assaulted, my father who murdered,' accused Donna Anna in the version of *Don Giovanni* prepared by Professor Edward Dent, a member of the Covent Garden board. English, many felt, sounded ridiculous in Italian opera. As its natural mode of delivery was drawled, an artificial enunciation had to be devised for the clipped consonants of *Il Trovatore*. In *Der Rosenkavalier*, at the other extreme, the slurred Viennese dialect had no close equivalent in English speech. Then there was the advertising issue: should *La Traviata* be billed by the name that audiences knew, or would the hoardings announce *The Wayward One* or *The Foundling*? These and related controversies rage on unresolved. For those dedicated to opera in the original tongue, there were regular relays and recordings on the BBC's Third Programme, and Glyndebourne filled the summer months with a festival of unaltered Mozart and Strauss.

The driving force behind Covent Garden's regeneration was John Maynard Keynes, the most influential living economist, a Cambridge scholar who became besotted with the stage while courting his ballerina wife, Lydia Lopokova. As head of the infant Arts Council and adviser to successive governments, Keynes tied up the legal and financial ribbons to form a new national company, specifically excluding all previous power-brokers. This meant no role for Glyndebourne's John Christie, whom Keynes had hated since they were schoolboys together at Eton. Also shut out, much to his chagrin, was Beecham, whom Keynes rightly feared would try to dominate the opera house in his own capricious way as he had done before both wars.

Devoid of operatic experience, the new company relied heavily in its opening phase on the balletic allure of Margot Fonteyn and her good companions. It was with *Sleeping Beauty*, not *Mastersingers*, that Covent Garden awoke on 20 February 1946 from its years of stagnation. Keynes, just as he was about to be presented to the King and Queen on a triumphant opening night, suffered a heart attack that proved fatal.

He had made a crucial final decision to release the company from the whims of free-spending musicians and social freeloaders and consign its management to a thrifty cloth trader. David Webster, who ran Covent Garden for a quarter of a century, was a Liverpool department-store executive with a profound attachment to his local orchestra and a provincial suspicion of metropolitan profligacy.

He was offered the grandiose and expensive Bruno Walter as musical director, but opted for a less charismatic Austrian refugee, the obscure Karl Rankl, who applied himself to building up an orchestra and chorus from scratch with whatever talent he could recruit out of army fatigues. Rankl, a modest, friendly musician and former pupil of Arnold Schoenberg, was transformed by the magnitude of his task into a seething bundle of resentments. He lacked the guile to haggle with Webster and the charm to socialize with the coalition of *aficionados* and intellectuals who ruled the governing board. His orchestra was the jewel of the house and played so sweetly for guest conductors that the directors dispensed with Rankl's services in 1951 and denied him any credit for his achievement. Covent Garden came of age that year with Erich Kleiber's performance of *Der Rosenkavalier* and Britten's *Billy Budd*.

With Rankl's dismissal, idealism gave way to opportunism. The 'snob-resistant' Keynes was succeeded as chairman by a former Conservative Chancellor of the Exchequer, Lord Waverley, who cared little for opera but knew how to squeeze cash out of the Treasury. He, in turn, was followed as chairman by the eleventh Earl of Drogheda, proprietor of the *Financial Times* and a mighty figure in the City. Moneymen and blue-bloods trickled back on to the board and the democratic concept of opera-for-all faded into the plush background. The most expensive seat in 1949 cost nineteen

Margot Fonteyn, stalwart of Covent Garden.

shillings; the current top ticket price is £120.

The need for more money at the box-office and wherever it could be found was inextricably linked to the gradual abandonment of Covent Garden's founding principles. For three years after Rankl's departure the directors wooed Kleiber and dangled carrots before Britten, who keenly desired the post of music director. When Kleiber proved too expensive and Britten politically too contentious, they turned to Rafael Kubelik, exiled from Czechoslovakia after the communist *putsch* of 1948 and recently chased from Chicago by poisonous critics. He was appointed on the strength of a sensational Janáček production at Sadler's Wells and responded with a memorable *Bartered Bride* and a revelatory

Dialogues of the Carmelites. Nationalist to the core, and as much a symbol of Czech freedom as Tomáš Masaryk had been, Kubelik supported the company's goal of singing in English with English singers and was stung into premature resignation when doubters, prompted by the meddlesome Beecham, cast aspersions on their collective quality. Kubelik, it was reckoned, was too sensitive for the hurly-burly of English public life.

No one would hurl that charge at his successor, the bull-headed Georg Solti, who was nicknamed the 'Screaming Skull' for his frequent tantrums. Solti, who had raised the opera companies of Munich and Frankfurt from post-war ruination, was not in the least interested in English aims and imperatives. He saw himself running an international company that would outstrip Vienna and La Scala. His decade contained a galaxy of historic events – Otto Klemperer's staging of *Fidelio*, the Callas-Gobbi *Tosca*, Britten's *Midsummer Night's Dream* and the first British performance of Schoenberg's *Moses und Aron*, complete with a stark-naked orgy around the golden calf. Joan Sutherland and Gwyneth Jones burst forth to world stardom, and Covent Garden became a pillar of the operatic firmament.

In the course of its transition, however, it sacrificed both linguistic and national ideals, jettisoned its sense of family and became a clearing-house for star travellers. The change was made without promulgation or consultation. More damagingly, it came about without securing the political or corporate backing to pay for its presumption. The problems that Covent Garden has faced ever since are a consequence of this blunder.

Much criticism has been levelled at Solti's anxiety-ridden successors, Colin Davis and Bernard Haitink, for a progressive decline in the quality of performances to a point where, in the 1990s, we are fortunate if two productions in a season are of satisfactory standard. Davis stayed for fifteen years but Haitink threatened to resign almost from the day he took office. The disasters they endorsed were inevitable in a company that lacked a clear mandate for its activities.

What, for example, was Covent Garden aiming to achieve with the world première of Hans Werner Henze's *We Come to the River*, a 1976 commission which proclaimed that socialist revolution was the greatest work of art? Why was an Italian who never answered the telephone appointed associate chief producer? And why did each decade need a new *Ring* production, which invariably proved inferior to its predecessor, the last two having been created by the director of the Deutsche Oper of West Berlin? In what sense was Covent Garden playing a role at the prow of British art?

These criticisms and countless more were inevitable at a company that invested the cream of its energies in raising funds for ambitions that had no public endorsement. International opera could be staged, with varying degrees of success, at La Scala and Vienna, where the State footed the bill, or in New York, where the Met could always woo the widow of another billionaire. Covent Garden, though, existed in a society that was historically indifferent to opera and not wholly convinced of the necessity of subsidized art. Nor were the arts supportive of Covent Garden, when the quality of its output was uneven and its thirst for cash drained resources from more deserving companies. With current funding of almost £20 million a year for opera and ballet, it receives six times as much as all the London orchestras put together, yet makes a lesser impact on public consciousness either at home or abroad. Internal morale is unsteady and strikes are not infrequent.

In the 1990s, Covent Garden faces a 3-year closure for reconstruction; it cannot expect to emerge unchanged. The likely options are either merger with the more imaginative English National Opera (ENO) or a reduction of its season to a few months, regressing to the situation that prevailed at Covent Garden between the wars. This would be the saddest coda of all.

ENO's ascent mirrored Covent Garden's decline. The former Sadler's Wells company moved into rented accommodation at the Coliseum, off Trafalgar Square, to persist with demotic offerings of opera in English. Where polite society dressed up for Covent Garden, it wore designer jeans to the Coli. The productions were chic and often infuriating. Familiar operas were subjected to deconstructionist revisions to underline an imagined contemporary relevance. *Rigoletto* was set among the New York mafiosi. At times, though, the ENO treatment was stupendously successful. Handel's *Xerxes* was revitalized as a modern comic masterpiece; Prokofiev's *Love for Three Oranges* was billed as the first opera with smells; *A Lady Macbeth of Mtsensk* by Shostakovich was an international revelation. Triumphs were scored on astonishingly tight budgets. The production of a new Shakespearian opera in 1991 was allocated £65,000; its producer, Graham Vick, was allocated £600,000 for *Otello* in Berlin.

Its ingenuity brought directors of European houses running to ENO rather than to Covent Garden for shared productions. Its devotion to English singing, though, deterred many foreign tourists, and local support for the vernacular began to dwindle when sur-titled simultaneous translations appeared at Covent Garden. If ENO gave up English singing, the main distinction between the two companies would disappear. ENO administrators are privately concerned that this would remove the barrier to a merger in which their company would be consumed. Such fears, while not irrational, overlook the company's very real achievements. English National Opera does not need the English language to survive. It has found a public among West End theatre-goers and the uncommitted young, who could neither afford nor would presume to set foot in the forbidding premises of the Royal Opera House. With a young, female music director in Sian Edwards, the house will obviously continue to innovate; any union with Covent Garden's current die-hards would only breed stagnation.

The existence of two houses engenders creative rivalry and avoids the gloom that settles on Vienna, for example, when its one and only flagship is going through the doldrums. In London, one opera house is usually on a high while the other is struggling, and the two strike sparks off one another in much the same way as do the orchestras. There is no easy solution – not even a spare billion pounds – for London's operatic conundrum. The best hope is that creative friction between ENO and Covent Garden can regenerate both companies, each for its particular audience.

Of the vision of 1945, what remains is the enhanced appeal of British singers who, two generations later, formed the nucleus of a Bayreuth *Ring* and the salvation of Salzburg. The other legacy was a catalogue of operas that London composers were encouraged to write for local consumption. Britten, of course, needed no further stimulus after *Peter Grimes*. He premièred *The Turn of the Screw* at Venice and *Owen Wingrave* on television, while reserving most other first nights for his private festival at Aldeburgh. Hypersensitive to personal slurs, he surrounded himself on the Suffolk coast with trusted aides and had little direct influence on compatriot composers.

Walton, stung by Britten's rise, spent five years writing an opera in frank retaliation. *Troilus and Cressida* was ruined at Covent Garden by an incompetent conductor and lacked the spark to procure its subsequent redemption, as Walton wandered off into the sunset of his Italian island. Britten's quirky friend Michael Tippett rode pillion on his success with *The Midsummer Marriage*, a mystifying opera to his own libretto that no one could fathom. Its music possessed a disarming ingenuousness that won Tippett a cultish following. Four of his operas have been created at Covent Garden, but the uptake elsewhere has been sluggish. Tippett may well prove too eccentric for any but the English.

The next generation of composers had a mixed reception. Covent Garden put on *Taverner* by Peter Maxwell Davies with a commitment that delighted young audiences but did not extend to other composers. It pulled out of a commission to Harrison Birtwistle, whose monumental *Mask of Orpheus* passed fifteen years

Designs for Birtwistle's Mask of Orpheus.

later to the English National Opera, where it was received as one of the most imaginative works in modern music theatre. Despite rave reviews and a full house for the final showing, it vanished after six performances for the infuriating, inevitable reason of cost. Amsterdam, Salzburg and Vienna suggested a co-produced revival, but ENO could not raise its share of the funding and, with the death of Barry Anderson who assembled its electronic components, the opera may never be seen again.

Birtwistle returned five years later with *Gawain* at Covent Garden, an epic opera of Wagnerian scope that seemed tangibly close to genius and has been promised a prompt revival. London, though, was no longer as receptive to new operas as it was in Britten's day, and nursery schemes at both ENO and Covent Garden yielded embarrassing flops. The rising generation of composers has begun to take its operas elsewhere – Nigel Osborne to Glyndebourne, Robert Saxton to Opera North, Mark-Antony Turnage to Munich, George Benjamin to Paris, various others straight on to video. The catch-22 is that while London needs new operas, it cannot afford the price of failure, with a philistine pack of editors and politicians waiting to denounce the waste of public funds on worthless modernity. Without risk, as every musician knows, there is no art. Without investment in new opera, there will be no opera at all.

There is an alternative aspect to opera in London which is affected by none of the aforementioned issues and concerns. A hard core of the opera public goes to Covent Garden for one reason alone – to hear the sound of a sweet siren voice. Oblivious to the scenery, untroubled by orchestral timbre, they wait two hours in rapt anticipation of a mad scene or death aria from a favoured prima donna and erupt in acclaim as if this well-worn episode had vindicated their life's purpose.

It is easy to mock these nightingale-fanciers, less easy for studious opera-lovers to understand their fixation. In most instances, it seems to represent surrogate adoration of an idealized mother-figure; Melba and Callas attracted this kind of devotion, as did Judy Garland and Edith Piaf in the popular music hall. A lesser form of diva-worship involves a quasi-religious attachment to an ideal of tonal and spiritual purity; Jenny Lind and Elisabeth Schwarzkopf appeared angelic. The third variety, scarcest of all, is the opera singer who radiates sexual heat all the way up to the upper galleries, attracting followers like moths to a flame; Emmy

Destinn and Maria Jeritza were such *femmes fatales*. To men afflicted by any form of this obsession, opera holds no greater charm, indeed no other charm.

London has been a prime haven for diva-fanciers ever since Francesca Cuzzoni was pitted against Faustina Bordoni in Handel's time and supporters came to blows over their rival merits. Handel gave each the same number of arias in *Alessandro*, but collaboration became impossible when the ladies started pulling one another's hair and their fans responded in kind. In June 1726 the *British Journal* reported:

> On Tuesday night last, a great Disturbance happened at the Opera, occasioned by the Partisans of the Two Celebrated Royal Ladies, Cuzzoni and Faustina. The Contention at first was only carried on by Hissing on one Side, and Clapping on the other; but proceeded at length to Catcalls and great Indecencies: And notwithstanding the Princess Caroline was present . . .[21]

Late in the eighteenth century the rage was Mrs Billington, a comely pupil of the London Bach who became mistress of the Prince of Wales and acquired notoriety with the publication of her spurious erotic memoirs.[22] Sir Joshua Reynolds painted her none the less as Saint Cecilia, and Haydn was struck by her beauty and her tone. She removed herself to Naples, where her detested husband died in suspicious circumstances and she became the first English singer to sway Italian hearts. Returning home in the new century, she commanded record fees at Covent Garden until the arrival of a coloratura from Sinigaglia, Angelica Catalani by name, whose demands were so exorbitant that the company was forced to raise its ticket prices, provoking riots in the process. Catalani was said to receive 200 guineas just for singing 'God Save the King' and 'Rule, Britannia!'

Giuditta Pasta, inamorata of the composer Bellini, was London's next top soprano, but the phenomenon of diva fever truly took off with Maria Malibran, daughter of Rossini's first Count Almaviva and victim of an ill-starred lovelife. Wasted in marriage to a businessman who sequestered all her earnings, she lived in sin with the Belgian violinist Charles de Bériot and invested her roles with a romantic torment, the like of which would not be heard again until Callas. What she lacked in vocal serenity, she made up for with the ferocious intensity of her acting, which transfixed men and women alike, among them George Sand and Bellini, who wrote *I Puritani* with her passion in mind. She sang many of her roles in English and, on her final appearance at Covent Garden, starred in both *Fidelio* and *La Sonnambula*. In the spring of 1836 she fell from a horse in Hyde Park and was concussed. Months later, in Manchester, she defied a headache to out-sing a rival soprano, collapsed in the dressing room and died the next day, aged twenty-eight.

The 'Swedish Nightingale', Jenny Lind, reigned supreme in the

The 'Swedish Nightingale' in Robert le Diable.

early years of Queen Victoria, blessed by the benediction of Mendelssohn and beatified for a personal life that was as blameless – that is to say, sexless – as her serene appearances on stage. She was, moreover, devoutly Protestant and devoid of Marian heresies.

An illegitimate and desperately unhappy child of the frozen North, she was the toast of Berlin and Vienna before reaching London on 4 May 1847 as Alice in Meyerbeer's *Robert le Diable*. The Queen, Prince Albert, the entire Cabinet and most of the diplomatic corps turn out to see her dragged on to the stage of Her Majesty's Theatre in a pilgrim's dress and clinging to a huge cross. The demand for tickets was so intense that a 'Jenny Lind crush' developed at the box-office and *The Times* reported 'torn dresses and evening coats reduced to rags; ladies fainting in the pressure and even gentlemen carried out senseless'.[23]

> Oh! is there not a pretty fuss
> In London all around,
> About the Swedish Nightingale
> The talk of all the town?

So rhymed a piece of popular doggerel entitled 'The Jenny Lind Mania'.[24] Her most constant admirer was the doddery Duke of Wellington, Napoleon's victor at Waterloo, who sat in his box at all her performances 'like an old, faithful dog', in Frédéric Chopin's poignant phrase.

Two years after her début, on 10 May 1849, and in the same role of Alice, Jenny Lind took her final bow on the operatic stage. At twenty-nine years old she retired in a sanctimonious halo and spent the rest of her days singing concerts and oratorios, drawing 6-figure rewards from the American circus-master P. T. Barnum and donating much of it to charity. She married her piano accompanist, Otto Goldschmidt, and was buried in the heart of an England that revered her almost as much as its monarch. She is commemorated in Poets' Corner in Westminster Abbey, beneath the bust of Handel and above his immortalized words, 'I know that my Redeemer liveth.'

Opera-swooners reverted for the rest of the century to an Italian queen, 'Sweet Adeline', whose theme-song 'Home, Sweet Home' reduced Victorian admirals to blubbing little boys. 'There is only one Niagara, and there is only one Patti,'[25] declared Jenny Lind on hearing her at Covent Garden, where she was a perennial fixture from 1861 to 1886 – an era known to its historians as 'the age of Patti'.

Nothing flustered Patti. Born in the middle of an opera when her heavy-bellied mother was caught short singing *Norma* in Madrid, she was umbilically attached to the stage. 'Give me only a dramatic idea with music that aids in depicting it and I will play you any part you choose, from one of Sarah Bernhardt's down to Fatima in *Bluebeard*,'[26] she told a journalist. When her sleeve caught fire on a footlight, she tore it off and stamped out the flame without missing a beat of her aria. Her life was carefully regimented to preserve good vocal health and she hardly ever cancelled a performance, except when an impresario was late in paying her extravagant fee. The wealth she amassed bought her a young third husband and a castle in Wales.

She was neither beautiful nor sexually alluring but possessed a rock-like security of tone and certainty of purpose. The same attributes were shared by her indomitable successor, Nellie Mitchell, who took as her stage-name the first syllable of her native city of Melbourne. Melba ruled Covent Garden with a rod of iron and tore a strip off Beecham when he had 'her' dressing room repainted without letting her choose the colour. She insisted on being paid more than anyone else, and received in guineas what

Patti raises the roof.

Caruso collected in pounds (1 guinea = 21 shillings, £1 = 20s). Melba Mania was more restrained that previous diva manifestations, but no less widespread. Chef Escoffier at the Savoy was among her most fervent fans and it was he who named after her the dessert known as 'Pêche Melba'. At Covent Garden they queued all night for tickets and she held a male audience in thrall until well into her sixties. 'A splendid woman,'[27] was the phrase that best described her. Melba, wrote Beecham laconically, 'was a singer who had *nearly* all the attributes inseparable from great artistry'.[28]

Despite gusting visits by Tetrazzini, Flagstad, Schwarzkopf and Callas, there was no single figure so commanding of Covent Garden's loyalty after Melba's departure – until, one night in 1959, a fellow-Australian, Joan Sutherland, erupted as if from nowhere in

Joan Sutherland in her breakthrough performance of Lucia's mad scene.

the title-role of Donizetti's *Lucia di Lammermoor*. Sutherland had been part of the company for seven years, creating a role in Tippett's *Midsummer Marriage* and serving in a variety of secondary functions. Callas, who once specialized in mad scenes and was nearing the end of her short tether, was in the audience that night, murmuring deprecatory remarks to her neighbour, Schwarzkopf. The galleries, though, knew a star had been born and serenaded 'La Stupenda' for the next thirty years. One critic exclaimed, 'God, she's as dull as Melba!'[29] but histrionic subtlety had little to do with the emotional grip that a great voice could exert on sections of her besotted audience. Sutherland's retirement in 1990 was mourned as the passing of an era, the end of a chain of titanic personalities.

Present infatuations pertain, with less obvious cause, to the persona of Kiri te Kanawa and the whooping delivery of Jessye Norman. Both are seen (and heard) to best advantage on television, but the house is packed whenever they appear, and their followers give every indication of sublime satisfaction no matter what, or how, they sing.

As a prophet is without honour in his own land, so is a native-born diva in London. Affectionate respect may be accorded to an occasional mezzo – Clara Butt, Kathleen Ferrier or Janet Baker – though more in token of their oratorios and *Lieder* than their static operatic performances. The perceived place of an English singer has traditionally been on the recital platform, rather than the dramatic stage, and those who presumed to full-blown soprano-hood were generally ignored by the indigenous *cognoscenti*. Maggie Teyte was lionized in Paris and Eva Turner in Milan; Gwyneth Jones is treasured in Vienna more than she ever has been in London; and the stock of Josephine Barstow began to rise only when Herbert von Karajan recruited the Coliseum staffer for key roles at Salzburg. As Germany ran out of Brünnhildes and Rhine maidens, Bayreuth came to London in the mid-1980s to recruit for its *Rings*, but the domestic attitude persisted that it was somehow 'not proper' for a nice English girl to put herself about in a big operatic role.

For reasons never fully apparent – but perhaps because they inherited the ridicule attached to ancient castrati – tenors never aroused the same passions as the divas of the day. Mario, the prince of bel canto, was virtually resident in London during the mid-nineteenth century, and Jean de Reszke and Enrico Caruso adorned Covent Garden during the Golden Age, but none was mobbed by admirers as they were in New York and Paris. While a diva's word was law, a tenor was never taken entirely seriously, although Pavarotti and Domingo nourished large fan clubs and thousands flocked to hear them sing in the open air, no matter how foul the weather.

Luciano Pavarotti arrived at Covent Garden in 1963, and Placido Domingo in 1971. The Italian was taken under the wing of the Decca record company, and the Spaniard that of the house management. The psychology of their popular appeal will doubtless be analysed when the memory of 1980s' excesses is less immediately acute. In artistic terms, it merely confirms Johnson's assumption that opera in London was, and is, an exotic and essentially irrational entertainment. 'People are wrong when they say opera isn't what is used to be,' quipped the playwright Noël Coward in 1933. 'It is what it used to be. That's what's wrong with it.'[30]

PART TWO

6

———

CHRONOLOGY

MUSIC IN LONDON FROM THE TIME OF JULIUS CAESAR TO THE PRESENT DAY

All performances listed are world premières, unless otherwise specified

[43   Roman legions make camp at Londinium.]

[193   A wall is built around the city.]

597   St Augustine, landing in Kent, brings Christianity and plain-song to Canterbury; they take years to reach London.

10th century   Church singers experiment with two-part harmonies.

[1066   Norman Conquest of England.]

1189–99   Reign of Richard the Lionheart, crusader and minstrel king. The legend of his rescue from captivity by a musician, Blondel de Nesle, inspired operas by André Grétry (1784) and William Shield (1786).

c. 1250   *Sumer is icumen in*, one of England's earliest surviving secular songs, is written, probably at Reading.

c. 1280   The Chapel Royal is formed at Edward I's Court, a body of clergy, choirmen and boys who provide devotional music for the monarch – the first government involvement in music.

[1348   Half of London's populace perishes in the Black Death.]

1381   The Peasants' Revolt marches on London and meets the

Early manuscript of Sumer is icumen in.

King at Mile End, where the rebel leader, Wat Tyler, is slain. He is commemorated in an opera by Alan Bush.

1453 John Dunstable, English composer whose music influenced Guillaume Dufay and the dominant Franco-Flemish school, is buried on Christmas Eve at St Stephen's Walbrook, near

Mansion House in the City. This is virtually the only verified fact of his life.

1469 Henry VI grants a royal charter to the Musicians' Guild.

1471 The Duke of Milan's *maestro di cappella* comes to London to recruit singers for his master's choir.

[1476 William Caxton sets up a printing press at Westminster.]

[1485 Richard III is killed in battle at Bosworth Field; Henry VII founds the Tudor dynasty.]

1493 1 January: William Newark is paid £1 from the royal purse for writing a song.

1494 The composer William Cornyshe is jailed in Fleet Prison for libelling a lawyer in his poem, 'A Treatise between Truth and Information'.

1502 25 December: Cornyshe is paid the sum of 13s 4d for 'setting a caralle on Christmas Day'.

1509 April: Henry VIII, minor composer inordinately devoted to music and matrimony, ascends the throne and conducts the reformation of English Christianity. He is the hero of an opera by Camille Saint-Saëns; his executed second queen, Anne Boleyn, stars in a Donizetti drama.

1514 John Taverner of Lincoln, first of the Tudor three Ts – Taverner, Christopher Tye, Thomas Tallis – spends time in the capital. He is suspected of being a government spy.

1516 Cornyshe, whose attention is not monopolized by music, wins a contract to supply lead urinals for the Whitsun festival at Greenwich.

1537 Thomas Tallis, 32, is organist at St Mary-at-Hill, Billingsgate.

1543 Tallis joins the Chapel Royal, mellifluously serving five monarchs and two conflicting faiths over the next 42 years.

1544 7 October: Thomas Cranmer, Archbishop of Canterbury, prescribes that songs for the new Anglican service should 'not be full of notes but, as near as may be, for every syllable a note, that it may be sung distinctly and devoutly'.

[1558 Six months after ordering herself a green satin-and-velvet set of virginals to ease her troubled soul, Bloody Queen Mary dies at the age of 42 and church bells joyfully ring out the accession of her half-sister, Elizabeth I.]

1562   Alfonso Ferrabosco, a canny Bolognese, joins Elizabeth's retinue as composer and, probably, undercover agent on his repeated trips to Italy. His canzonettas, madrigals and motets leave their mark on English colleagues.

1572   William Byrd, 29, arrives from Lincoln, where he was cathedral organist.

1573   Tallis writes a 40-part motet *Spem in alium* for Elizabeth's 40th birthday.

1574   John Bull, aged 11, joins the Chapel Royal.

1575   Elizabeth grants Byrd, an unreformed Catholic, and his teacher Tallis exclusive rights to print and import music. Their first collection is a sequence of melancholic, polyphonic *Cantiones sacrae*.

1577   Expenses running high, they apply for – and receive – State subsidy; Byrd migrates to the Middlesex village of Harlesden.

1578   Ferrabosco is fired after an unexplained murder. He leaves in Greenwich a son of the same name, who turns out to be an even finer composer.

1585   Tallis dies in his 80th year at Greenwich. He is buried at St Alphege parish church beneath the epitaph:

> As he did lyve
> so also did he dy
> in myld and quyet sort (O, happy man).

1587   Mary Queen of Scots is executed on Elizabeth's orders. She is the tragic heroine of two dozen operas, far outperforming her victorious cousin on the musical stage (Donizetti wrote the outstanding *Maria Stuarda*, Rossini the reigning *Elisabetta*).

1588   As the Spanish Armada sails to avenge martyred Mary,

London dances to a new anthology of Italian madrigals, mostly by Luca Marenzio.

1592   John Dowland, 29, a dolorous lutenist, plays for Elizabeth but, failing to find favour, takes a job at the Court of Denmark.

c. 1592   William Shakespeare makes his name in the London theatre. Much original music was written for his plays, notably Thomas Morley's 'It was a lover and his lass' from *As You Like It* and Robert Johnson's 'Where the bee sucks' from *The Tempest*.

1597   John Bull, 34, Reader in Music at Gresham College, is the first academic to lecture in English instead of Latin. A brilliant and popular keyboard virtuoso, he is renowned – in the Archbishop of Canterbury's immortal phrase – as much 'for marring of virginity as he is for fingering of organs and virginals'.

1598   Thomas Morley, organist of St Paul's, issues a *Plaine and Easie Introduction to Practicall Musicke.*

1600   Dowland's *Second Book of Ayres* is published, containing some of the Elizabethan era's finest songs.

[1603   Elizabeth dies. Her successor, Mary Stuart's son, James I, orders an English translation of the Bible.]

1603–4   Dowland takes a house in Fetter Lane, issues a *Third Book of Ayres* and the *Lachrymae* for viols, but cannot find work and returns to Denmark.

1605   Alfonso Ferrabosco the younger joins Ben Jonson to write masques – medleys of music, verse, dance and drama.

1607   Bull is sacked by the university after getting a girl pregnant; he plays at Court for six years until charges of adultery and brawling in church force him to flee to Brussels.

1612   October: Dowland is finally appointed lutenist to King James, his great talent now fast fading; Ferrabosco is made music master to young Prince Charles.

1613   Thomas Campion, physician, poet, lawyer, madrigalist,

John Bull.

publishes a significant treatise on counterpoint.

1623   4 July: Death of Byrd, aged 80. Orlando Gibbons becomes organist at Westminster Abbey.

1625   [Charles I succeeds his father, dissolves Parliament, leans towards Rome, and patronizes the painters Rubens and Van Dyck.]
5 June: Gibbons, 41, dies of a fever caught while waiting for the new Queen to arrive from France. His son, Christopher, sings with the Chapel Royal.

Orlando Gibbons.

1626   20 February: Dowland, 62, is buried at St Anne, Blackfriars.

1628   11 March: Ferrabosco II dies at Greenwich, aged about 47.

1634   Composer Henry Lawes provides music to a masque by the poet John Milton, who praises:

> Harry, whose tuneful and well-measured song
> First taught our English music how to span
> Words with just note and accent ...

[1642–9 Civil War between King and Parliament ends in Charles's capture and execution, and the promulgation of a Puritan republic under Oliver Cromwell. On 13 November 1642 an army of 24,000 Londoners forces the King's men to turn back at Turnham Green.]

1645   24 September: William Lawes, 43, reputedly a better composer than his brother Henry, is killed in crossfire in the battle for Chester, fighting for the King.

1647   15 March: John Milton, composer of anthems and father of the poet, is buried at St Giles, Cripplegate.

1654   John Playford's *Breefe Introduction to the Skill of Musicke* becomes a standard text for the next century.

1656   September: The earliest English opera, a glorified masque entitled *The Siege of Rhodes*, is staged privately at Rutland House in Aldersgate Street, all theatres having been shut by the Puritan government. The text is by William Davenant, future Poet Laureate; the music, by Henry Lawes, Henry Cooke and Matthew Locke, has not survived.

1661   23 April: The restoration of Charles II lightens the cultural atmosphere; his coronation is celebrated by Lawes's setting of the anthem *Zadok the Priest*.

1663   The Theatre Royal in Drury Lane is one of several new stages to open; Nell Gwyn sells oranges there (and perhaps herself), catching the King's eye.

1664   Pelham Humfrey, 17, a 'pretty boy' in the Chapel Royal, is given £450 from secret-service funds to study in France and Italy, supposedly with Jean-Baptiste Lully and Giacomo Carissimi.

[1665–6   The Plague, followed by the Great Fire of London, destroys the medieval city and a quarter of its populace.]

1666   19 December: Samuel Pepys, senior civil servant, reports: 'Talked of the King's family [*sic*] with Mr Hingston, the organist. He says many of the musique are ready to starve, they being five years behindhand for their wages; nay, Evans, the famous man upon the harp, having not his equal in the world, did the other day die for mere want ...'

1668   John Blow, 19, is appointed organist at Westminster Abbey, a post he yields in 1679 to his pupil Henry Purcell and regains on his death in 1695. A key figure in the musical revival, he directs the choir at St Paul's and plays in the Chapel Royal.

1669   Purcell, aged 9, joins the boys' choir of the Chapel Royal.

1672   30 December: The world's first paid-entry public concerts are announced at John Banister's house, near the George Tavern, Whitefriars.

1673   The important French composer Robert Cambert, banished from Paris by Lully's monopoly at the Sun King's Court, stages a couple of operas in London but soon dies, possibly at the hands of a Lully agent.

1674   14 July: Weeks after supplying music for a spectacular production of Shakespeare's *The Tempest*, Pelham Humfrey dies unfulfilled at Windsor, aged just 26. Purcell, 14, his broken voice useless to the Chapel Royal, is appointed tuner of the organ at Westminster Abbey.

1677   At 18, Purcell is named 'composer to the King's violins'.

1678   Thomas Britton, a coal merchant in Clerkenwell, stages professional concerts in rooms above his business.

1680   Purcell starts composing for London theatres.

1683   22 November: For concerts on St Cecilia's Day, patron saint of music, Purcell contributes a peerless Ode.

[1685–8   Charles II proclaims himself Catholic on his deathbed; his brother, James II, veers towards Rome and is deposed by William of Orange.]

1688   Purcell is fined for selling seats in his organ loft to people wishing to watch William and Mary's coronation.

1689   Purcell's superb opera *Dido and Aeneas* is 'Perform'd at Mr Josias Priest's Boarding-School at Chelsey by Young Gentlewomen'.

1691   He collaborates with the poet John Dryden on *King Arthur*.

1692   Purcell composes *The Fairy Queen* after Shakespeare's *Midsummer Night's Dream*.

1695   21 November: After months of illness – and not, as the story has it, because he was locked out at night by his irate wife – Purcell dies at the age of 36. His brother Daniel succeeds him as composer to theatreland. No comparable talent arises in

England for two centuries.

1696 Blow and Dryden write *Ode on the Death of Mr Henry Purcell*.

1704–5 A London colony of immigrant musicians forms around the Flemish flautist-composer Jean-Baptiste Loeillet and the Prussian violist-composer Johann Christoph Pepusch, who seeks asylum after seeing his King summarily behead an officer – 'pour encourager les autres'.

1705 The Queen's Theatre (alternately the King's Theatre) on the Haymarket is erected by the dramatist-architect Sir John Vanbrugh and managed by the comedian William Congreve.

1707 1 December: Jeremiah Clarke, 33, organist at St Paul's and composer of the 'Trumpet Voluntary', shoots himself in the churchyard for love 'of a very beautiful lady of a rank far superior to his own'.

1710 November: The Elector of Hanover's Kapellmeister, Georg Friedrich Händel, aged 25, arrives in England.

1711 15 February: He presents *Rinaldo* at the Queen's Theatre. He writes a birthday ode for Queen Anne and returns home in May.

1712 October: Händel is back to revive *Rinaldo* and compose *Il Pastor Fido* and *Teseo*.

1713 13 January: Händel offers a *Te Deum* for the Treaty of Utrecht, a pact strongly opposed by his employer.
6 February: A second *Birthday Ode for Queen Anne* earns him a welcome annuity.

1714 1 August: On Anne's death, George, Elector of Hanover, becomes King of England. Händel quickly offers a *Te Deum*.

1717 17 July: His sparkling *Water Music* is designed to accompany the King's barge down the Thames. Happily settled in England, he anglicizes his name to George Frideric Handel and becomes composer in residence to the Duke of Chandos in Stanmore.

1719–20 The Royal Academy of Music asks him to travel through Europe in search of opera singers.

1720 14 November: Handel's first keyboard music is published.
19 November: Giovanni Bononcini's *Astarto* revives opera in

London after a 3-year interval.

1723   12 January: The sensational Francesca Cuzzoni debuts in Handel's *Ottone*.
25 February: Handel becomes 'Composer of Musick for His Majesty's Chapel Royal', moves to Lower Brook Street in the West End and crowns his operatic activity with:

1724   20 February: *Giulio Cesare*
31 October: *Tamerlano*

1725   13 February: *Rodelinda*, and numerous revivals and revisions of previous successes.

1726   5 May: Faustina Bordoni makes her mark in Handel's *Alessandro*, sparking a violent rivalry with Cuzzoni and her aristocratic supporters. Handel writes *Admeto*.

1727   20 February: He becomes a British citizen by Royal Assent. October: His anthem *Zadok the Priest* is performed at George II's coronation and at every subsequent enthronement to the present day.

1728   29 January: John Gay triumphs with *The Beggar's Opera*, a satire on *opera seria* consisting of 69 street songs and an overture by Pepusch. It runs for 63 nights at Lincoln's Inn Fields.
17 February: Handel stages *Siroe*.
30 April: He stages *Tolomeo* but his company collapses in June.

1730   8 August: Handel plays the new organ at Westminster Abbey.

1731   Bononcini departs in disgrace, having failed to answer charges that he plagiarized another man's madrigal.

1732   23 February: On his 47th birthday, Handel introduces a new concept, the dramatic oratorio *Esther*.

1732   May: Summer evening entertainments begin at Vauxhall Gardens.
7 December: With profits from *The Beggar's Opera*, impresario John Rich opens Covent Garden theatre.

1733   Handel composes *Deborah* and *Athalia* for a new company, the Opera of the Nobility, at Lincoln's Inn.

1734   Farinelli, the great castrato, hogs the limelight at Lincoln's Inn. Handel moves over to Covent Garden.

1736   19 February: He presents *Alexander's Feast*, to Dryden's text.

1737   April: Shortly before staging *Berenice*, Handel suffers a stroke that leaves his right hand partially paralysed. His season ends with a £10,000 deficit.
December: He writes a Funeral Anthem, then composes the dazzling comedy *Xerxes*.

1738   1 May: A statue of Handel (by Louis Roubiliac) is erected in Vauxhall Gardens.
September–October: Handel composes *Saul* and *Israel in Egypt*.

1739   22 November: Handel writes his own *Ode for St Cecilia's Day*, to Dryden's text.

1740   1 August: Thomas Arne's masque *Alfred*, staged at Cliveden, ends with his rousing anthem 'Rule, Britannia!', rallying-cry of the expanding empire.

1741   Handel composes *Messiah* but takes it to Dublin.

1743   18 February: *Samson* at Covent Garden.
23 March: Almost a year after its first performance, *Messiah* comes to London. Handel suffers a second stroke. He nevertheless composes *Semele* and a *Te Deum* for George II's victory over the French at Dettingen.

1744   Handel's 24 subscription concerts are sabotaged by a section of the nobility.

1745   28 September: Anxiety over the Jacobite Rebellion results in a spontaneous eruption of 'God Save the King' by actors at Drury Lane, led by Arne at the head of the orchestra. The song is taken up at other theatres and becomes the national anthem.

1746   January: As the rebels reach Derby, the visiting composer Christoph Willibald von Gluck supports the Hanoverians with his opera *La Caduta de' Giganti* (*Fall of the Giants*); he earns Handel's scorn.

1747   1 April: Handel hails George II's 'Conqu'ring hero' in *Judas Maccabaeus* at Covent Garden. He then composes *Joshua*.

1748   Handel composes *Solomon* and *Susanna*.

1749   27 April: *Music for the Royal Fireworks* is performed at Green Park to celebrate peace in Europe. François-André Danican Philidor, known in Paris as an opera composer, issues in London

Announcement of the first London performance of Handel's Messiah.

his *L'Analyze des échecs*, an unbeatable guide to chess-playing, of which he is uncrowned British champion.

1750 May: *Messiah* is performed for the benefit of the Foundling Hospital, on which Handel lavishes charitable concern. He sends the ailing Georg Telemann a Christmas gift of rare plants and treats himself to a large Rembrandt.

1751 February: While writing *Jephtha*, Handel loses the sight of one eye.

1753 Completely blind, he starts giving public organ recitals.

1754 31 January: Philidor sets Congreve's *Ode to Music* for the Haymarket; Handel considers it well-written but tasteless.

1755 William Boyce, 45, becomes Master of the King's Musick.

1757 Benjamin Franklin, amateur composer, inventor of the glass harmonica and founding father of the United States, settles in Craven Street, off the Strand, for the next 18 years.

1758 A German composer, Carl Friedrich Abel, moves to London.

1759 14 April: At 8 a.m. Handel dies at his home in Brook Street. 20 April: He is buried in Westminster Abbey before a congregation of 3,000.

1760 [George III ascends the throne.]
Boyce publishes Eight Symphonies.
Appearance of the world's first music biography, the Rev. John Mainwaring's *Memoirs of the Life of Handel*.

1762 Johann Christian Bach, 11th and youngest son of Johann Sebastian, arrives in London with a commission to write two operas for the King's Theatre.

1763 March: He dedicates an Op. 1 set of concertos to the German-born Queen Charlotte, advertises himself as her music master and becomes known as 'the London Bach'.

1764 26 February: Bach and Abel give a joint concert.
23 April: Wolfgang Amadeus Mozart, aged 8, arrives with his father, mother and sister for a 15-month stay.
24 April: They find lodgings with a barber, John Couzin, at 19 Cecil Court, Leicester Square. The boy performs three times for the King and Queen and plays duets with Bach.
5 August: When Leopold Mozart falls seriously ill, the family moves to the fresher air of Chelsea where, at 180 Ebury Street, Wolfgang writes his first symphony (K.16). 'Remind me to give the horns something good to do,' he tells his sister.

1765 23 January: Bach and Abel announce the world's first subscription series, a season of 10 concerts at Carlisle House, Soho Square. Sadler's Wells, a musical theatre, opens at Islington.

1770 Charles Burney, organist and composer, sets out on a European trip to research his history of music.

1774 Muzio Clementi, 22, impresses with his keyboard playing. 28 June: Bach, Abel and G. A. Gallini invest (and lose) £5,000 in a site on Hanover Square, which they open on 1 February 1775 as a new concert hall.

1776   [US War of Independence.]
In the race to publish an English history of music, the first of Charles Burney's four volumes appears nine months before John Hawkins's complete work.

1778   Thomas Gainsborough paints Bach's portrait.

1779   7 February: Boyce, 67, dies of gout and is buried beneath the dome of St Paul's. He is succeeded as Master of the King's Musick by the blind organist John Stanley, 59.
26 February: Philidor gives three performances of his setting of Horace's *Carmen seculare*, earning £450 in receipts and 5,000 livres from the Russian Empress, Catherine II.

1781   23 March: Johann Peter Salomon, an enterprising German violinist, makes his début at Covent Garden – but has bolder plans.
J. C. Bach, in failing health, moves from Richmond to Paddington 'for a change of air'.

1782   1 January: He dies there, aged 46, with debts of £4,000, and is buried in St Pancras Churchyard.
William Herschel, a musician from Hanover, having discovered the planet Uranus while playing at Bath, is named Astronomer Royal and constructs a 40-foot telescope at Slough.

1784   26–9 May: A royal commemoration of Handel with 513 performers, 'on such a scale of magnificence as could not be equalled in any part of the world', draws crowds to Westminster Abbey and becomes an annual event.

1785   616 performers join the Handel centenary commemoration.
24 April: Luigi Cherubini, 24, makes his name with *La finta Principessa (The fake princess)*.

1789   [French Revolution.]
8 June: Philidor's *Ode on His Majesty's Recovery* (known in France as *Ode Anglaise*) marks a brief respite in George III's advancing insanity.
24 November: Stephen Storace, Mozart's friend, presents *The Haunted Tower*, a horror-opera.

1790   Among many refugees from the French Revolution is Jan

Ladislav Dussek, the Bohemian pianist and publisher.

1791 1 January: Joseph Haydn, 58, arrives in London to perform in Salomon's new series of concerts at Hanover Square.
11 March: The first Haydn series of 12 concerts opens with his 96th symphony. Clementi fails with a rival season.
May–June: A record 1,068 musicians take part in the ultimate Handel commemoration, among them Johann Nepomuk Hummel.
June: Haydn takes as a pupil, and falls in love with, Rebecca Schroeter, a composer's widow.

1792 14 January: A scurrilous biography of soprano Elizabeth Billington sells out by 3 p.m. on the day of publication. Haydn, who considers her 'a great Genius', is appalled.
17 February: Haydn premières his 93rd symphony to great acclaim. The first of 12 London Symphonies is followed by:
24 February: *The Storm* chorus
2 March: the 98th symphony
9 March: Sinfonia concertante
23 March: the *Surprise* (94th) and
3 May: at his benefit concert, the 97th.
15 June: Haydn goes to Slough to see Herschel's great telescope.
end June: Haydn departs.

1793 February: War between England and France cuts Philidor off from his family. He is declared an illegal émigré in Paris and faces death if he attempts to return.
7 February: Giovanni Battista Viotti, famed violinist who fled the French Revolution, makes a stunning début at Hanover Square. Among eight concertos he writes in London is the 22nd in A minor, admired by Brahms, who quotes from it in his D-major violin concerto (1878).
December: Lorenzo da Ponte, Mozart's librettist, now destitute, is appointed Poet to the King's Theatre.
Clementi takes an 11-year-old Irish pupil, John Field.

1794 4 February: Haydn returns. He introduces:
10 February: his 99th symphony
3 March: The *Clock* (101st)
31 March: The *Military* (100th).
October: Viotti is named acting manager of the King's Theatre, the leading operatic stage. He turns it into a popular concert venue in a merger with Haydn and Salomon.

1795   1 February: Haydn plays piano and sings a selection of his own works at a soirée for the mad King, 'who hitherto could or would only hear Handel's music'.
2 February: He directs his 102nd symphony with the 60-piece orchestra assembled by Viotti, who plays a new concerto.
2 March: His *Drumroll* (103rd) 'excites the deepest attention'.
4 May: The London Symphony, his 104th and last, is performed at Haydn's benefit concert.
15 August: Refusing royal offers of lodgings at Windsor, Haydn returns home to Vienna. His pupils report that the days in England were 'the happiest of his life'.
31 August: Poor Philidor, 68, dies alone in his lodgings at 10 Little Ryder Street and is buried off Hampstead Road.

1796   18 March: Storace dies of pneumonia, at 33.

1798   4 March: The celebrated Viotti is expelled from England accused of revolutionary sympathies, a charge apparently trumped up by rival musicians. He retreats for three years to Hamburg, where he writes remarkable violin duets for his London friends Mr and Mrs George Chinnery, 'some dictated by pain, others by hope'.
Clementi founds a music-publishing and piano-making firm.

1800   To escape a wild bull rampaging down the Strand, Lorenzo da Ponte takes refuge in a bookshop at 5 Pall Mall and, after talking with the proprietor, buys the store. Michael Kelly, the Irish tenor who sang in the first *Marriage of Figaro*, opens a competing business across the Mall.

1801   18 February: Viotti's expulsion order is lifted; he returns, giving up music for some years in favour of the wine trade.

1805   7 April: Da Ponte emigrates to America.

1806   23 March: Tragic death of George Frederick Pinto, aged 20, a remarkably promising piano composer and 'martyr to dissipation'; he is buried at St Margaret's Westminster.

1808   19 September: Covent Garden theatre burns down; it reopens within a year.
Samuel Wesley, nephew of the founder of the Methodist faith, revives the music of J. S. Bach, whom he calls 'Saint Sebastian'.

1809   24 February: All traces of Henry Bishop's *Circassian Bride* go up in flames in the burning down of Drury Lane theatre.

1810   27 November: Francesco Bianchi, Italian opera composer, kills himself in Hammersmith.

1811   Vincent Novello starts a music-publishing dynasty in Soho.

1812   Samuel Chappell founds a company of music publishers, piano-makers and concert promoters.

1813   24 January: Five musicians meeting at 17 Manchester Street form a Philharmonic Society to give regular concerts.
8 March: Its first event is at the Argyll Rooms, on the present-day site of Oxford Circus Underground station.

1814   Beethoven appeals to London musicians to stop pirate performances of his Battle Symphony by Johann Nepomuk Maelzel, inventor of the metronome.

1815   [Napoleon defeated at Waterloo.]
The Canterbury composer Isaac Nathan sells Lord Byron some Hebrew melodies allegedly sung at Solomon's Temple.

1817   9 June: The Philharmonic Society invites Beethoven to London to compose and perform two symphonies for a fee of 300 guineas. He cannot face the journey.

1820   10 April: Ludwig Spohr, German composer, rehearsing his third concert, raises the first baton ever seen on an English podium. His 4th (1835), 5th (1840), 6th (1840) and 8th (1848) symphonies have their premières in London.

1822   The Royal Academy of Music, London's first conservatory, opens in Tenterden Street; William Crotch is founder-principal.

1823   7 December: Rossini arrives for a 6-month stay. He fails to deliver a promised opera but soaks the aristocracy for £7,000 with revamped works and overpriced music lessons.

1824   3 March: Viotti, 78, dies at the Marylebone home of Mrs Chinnery, to whom he bequeathes his Stradivarius.
21 June: Franz Liszt, 12, makes his UK début.

1825   21 March: The Philharmonic Society gives the UK première of the 9th symphony it commissioned from Beethoven.

1826   12 April: Carl Maria von Weber presents *Oberon* to a feeble
English libretto at Covent Garden.
5 June: He is found dead in bed of consumption, aged 39.

1827   28 February: Learning that Beethoven is ill and penniless in
Vienna, the Philharmonic Society sends £100 'to be applied to
his comforts and necessities'. He dies a month later.

1829   Mendelssohn, 18, on his first visit, introduces Beethoven's
Emperor Concerto, making such an impression that he is
elected the first honorary member of the Philharmonic Society.
On an excursion to Scotland he writes the famous *Hebrides* overture and Scottish Symphony.

1831   14 May: Niccolò Paganini, 48, on his first UK tour, sends
Mary Shelley into hysterics, earns £10,000 and starts a 3-year
affair with Charlotte Watson, aged 16.

1832   10 March: Clementi expires at 80 and finds a spot in the
Abbey.

1833   26 April: Vincenzo Bellini supervises local productions of
La Sonnambula, Il Pirata, Norma and *I Capuleti e i Montecchi*.
29 April: Among the King's Theatre audience for *La Cenerentola*
are Mendelssohn, Paganini, Hummel and Bellini.
13 May: Mendelssohn conducts his Italian Symphony for the
Philharmonic Society; in the same concert he directs Mozart's
D-minor concerto (K.466) from the keyboard.
14 May: Paganini plays the viola in the world première of his
Trio Concertante, with Mendelssohn playing the guitar part on
the piano, and Robert Lindley as the cellist.

1836   Charles Dickens marries Catherine, daughter of music
critic George Hogarth, and writes an opera, *The Village
Coquettes*, with a young composer, John Hullah.
July: Chopin visits, incognito and unheard, to see the sights.

1838   28 June: Johann Strauss the elder stands outside the Reform
Club leading his band in 'God Save the Queen' on Coronation
Day, and at Buckingham Palace plays *Homage to Queen Victoria*.

THE IVY GREEN.
Written by Charles Dickens Esq.
Composed by
HENRY RUSSELL.

LONDON. D'ALMAINE & C? SOHO SQUARE.
The Words of this Song are Published by the express permission of the Author Charles Dickens Esq.

He writes a further waltz for Victoria's wedding to Prince Albert of Saxe-Coburg.

1839   12 August: Wagner, 26, disembarks with wife and dog at London Bridge, 'the unique centre of this immense, densely packed universe'.

1840   Summer: A penniless French conductor, Louis Jullien, introduces 'promenade concerts' of popular music interspersed with classic works.

1841   Isaac Nathan heads for the Antipodes, where he becomes known as 'Father of Australian Music'.

1842   13 May: Arthur Sullivan is born at 8 Bolwell Street, Lambeth, son of an Irish military bandmaster.

1843   27 November: Michael William Balfe's *The Bohemian Girl* runs for 100 nights.

1844   March: Mendelssohn conducts 13-year-old Hungarian violinist Joseph Joachim in music by Heinrich Wilhelm Ernst and Ludwig Spohr and presents him to Queen Victoria. Joachim returns annually for the next six decades, exercising immense influence on London's musical climate.
Novello launches the monthly, *Musical Times.*

1845   John Ella, a violinist, forms a Musical Union to play chamber music concerts at the homes of wealthy patrons. A cycle of Beethoven quartets is given in Harley Street at the initiative of Thomas Alsager, a manager of *The Times*, which appoints its first music critic, James William Davison.

1846   10 August: Mendelssohn rehearses *Elijah* at Ignaz Moscheles's home, 3 Chester Place, Regent's Park. His oratorio triumphs at Birmingham but the composer dies within the year.

1847   22 July: Giuseppe Verdi, using a baton for the first time, conducts *I Masnadieri*, starring the 'Swedish Nightingale', Jenny Lind. One critic calls it 'the worst opera ever to have been given at Her Majesty's Theatre'.
5 November: Hector Berlioz arrives to conduct Jullien's company at Drury Lane, staying at his employer's house at 76 (now 27) Harley Street until bailiffs seize the premises in lieu of unpaid taxes. He conducts, *inter alia*, on 20 December, Balfe's new *Maid of Honour* and a Christmas pantomime.

1848   7 February: A concert of Berlioz's music at Drury Lane wins him many admirers. He leaves in June but returns repeatedly.
23 June: Consumptive Chopin, fleeing the revolution in Paris, gives his first UK public recital. He travels north when fees and pupils prove hard to find.
16 November: After a gruelling Scottish tour, Chopin gives the

last performance of his life, at the Guildhall, in aid of Polish refugees. He leaves on 23 November for Paris, where he dies 11 months later.

1851   1 May: A Great Exhibition opened by Queen Victoria in Hyde Park shows the triumphs of modern British invention; Berlioz judges the musical instruments – unfavourably. Six million people pass through the gates and profits of £180,000 endow part of the site in South Kensington as museums and music colleges. The exhibition's glass hall is removed to Sydenham as the Crystal Palace.

1852–3   A New Philharmonic Society is formed with Berlioz as conductor, designed to show up the conservatism of the existing society.

1854   10 June: Crystal Palace opens with an array of 1,700 performers and an audience of 30,000; an engineer, George Grove, is Secretary of its adventurous concerts.

1855   12 March: Wagner conducts eight concerts for the old Philharmonic Society. He is unfavourably compared to Berlioz, whose overture *Le Corsaire* is dedicated to *The Times's* critic.

1856   5 March: Covent Garden is destroyed again by fire. 'It is some time since we burnt down one of our national theatres,' reports *The Times*, 'but this oversight has been amply repaired this morning.'
14 April: Clara Schumann, 37 and mother of eight, forced by her husband's illness to earn a pianist's crust, makes her début in London where, with Joachim, she forms the focus of anti-Wagner prejudice. Her recital contains pieces by both Schumanns and one by their protégé Johannes Brahms.
The Royal Military School of Music opens at Kneller Hall, Twickenham, to train army bandsmen.

1858   15 May: The third (and present) opera house at Covent Garden (ROH) opens with Meyerbeer's *Les Huguenots*. A purpose-built concert venue, St James's Hall, is erected at a cost of £40,000 opposite the church of the same name in Piccadilly.

1859   25 July: Closing night at Vauxhall Gardens, where the trees are pulled down as developers move in.

1860   28 February: George Augustus Polgreen Bridgetower, Afro-Polish violinist for whom Beethoven wrote what became

The second burning of Covent Garden.

the Kreutzer Sonata – they performed it together but promptly fell out – dies in London obscurity, aged 81.

1861   Summer: Pyotr Ilyich Tchaikovsky, 21, arrives as a tourist, hates the weather but adores the cuisine: 'The dishes are simple – plain even – but filling and tasty.'

1862   May: Meyerbeer and Verdi perform new pot-boilers at the International Exhibition.
Winter: Naval cadet Nikolai Rimsky-Korsakov, 18, visits London while his ship is remasted at Gravesend, and starts composing his first symphony in E-flat minor.

1863   11 June: Gounod's *Faust* opens at Covent Garden, four years after the Paris première, and is revived unfailingly for the next 48 seasons.

1864   The Royal College of Organists opens in Kensington.

1866   10 March: An Irish Symphony by Arthur Sullivan, 24, is performed at Crystal Palace.

1867   16 August: Johann Strauss the younger begins two months of concerts, in the course of which he writes his *Memories of Covent Garden* waltz.

10 November: Schubert's complete music for *Rosamunde* is conducted by August Manns at Crystal Palace, after being found in a Vienna cupboard by Arthur Sullivan and George Grove.

1871   March: The Royal Albert Hall (RAH), commemorating Victoria's late Consort on the Hyde Park site of his Great Exhibition, opens to the sound of one of his own compositions. It seats up to 10,000.

1 May: Charles Gounod, a refugee from the Franco-Prussian War, writes a patriotic oratorio, *Gallia*, for the RAH.

19 June: Gounod takes refuge for the next three years at Tavistock House, Bloomsbury, home of Mrs Georgina Weldon, with whom he enjoys a violent relationship.

2 August: Anton Bruckner, unknown outside Austria, inaugurates the RAH organ with six recitals.

19 August: Bruckner gives four more recitals at Crystal Palace, playing for a crowd of 70,000. 'Unfortunately the critic of *The Times* is in Germany, so hardly anything will be written about me,' he laments.

26 December: The first Gilbert-and-Sullivan opera, *Thespis*, has a quiet reception.

1872   Sullivan writes the hymn 'Onward Christian soldiers'.

1875   Trinity College, now part of the University of London, becomes the second music conservatory.

25 March: *Trial by Jury* is the first Gilbert-and-Sullivan hit.

1876   26 April: The Bach Choir, formed by Otto Goldschmidt, gives the first British performance of the B-minor Mass.

1877   1 May: To recoup losses from the Bayreuth *Ring*, Wagner gives eight concerts at the RAH but emerges with barely £700.

1878   25 May: *HMS Pinafore* (G&S).

The People's Concert Society forms to provide Sunday music at low cost to the poorer districts.

1879   5 May: Wagner's conductor Hans Richter starts an annual concert series at St James's Hall.

Macmillan publishes the first volume (A to Impromptu) of George Grove's *Dictionary of Music and Musicians (A.D. 1450–1880) by Eminent Writers, English and Foreign, with Illustrations and Woodcuts*. Although 102 of its 118 contributors are British, it sets global standards.

Gilbert and Sullivan present *The Pirates of Penzance*.

1880 The City of London founds its own Guildhall School of Music and Drama.

1881 23 April: *Patience* (G&S) opens, moving, on 10 October, to Richard D'Oyly Carte's Savoy Theatre, the first London stage with electric lighting.

1882 18 April: The conductor Leopold Stokowski is born at 13 Upper Marylebone Street – not, as he maintained, at sundry other places and at later dates.

May: Wagner's *Ring* comes to Her Majesty's Theatre, conducted by Anton Seidl with Bayreuth singers.

25 November: *Iolanthe* (G&S).

1883 The Royal College of Music (RCM) is founded in Kensington, with Grove as director.

1885 14 March: Despite justified protests from the Japanese ambassador at its inherent racism and sadism, *The Mikado* (G&S) enjoys enormous acclaim at the Savoy.

22 April: Antonin Dvořák premières his 7th symphony – 'a work to shake the world' – for the Philharmonic Society.

1886 19 May: Camille Saint-Saëns conducts his 3rd and finest symphony, the Organ Symphony in C minor, for the Philharmonic Society.

Liszt pays a last visit to hear his *Legend of St Elisabeth*.

1887 27 June: Charles Villiers Stanford, professor at Trinity, performs his Irish Symphony.

1888 March: Tchaikovsky has such success with Serenade for Strings that the Philharmonic Society adds a £5 bonus to his £20 fee.

3 May: Edvard Grieg has a tumultuous London début: 'When I showed myself at the orchestra doorway, the whole of the vast St James's Hall, completely full, broke into an uproar, so intense and so continuous (I think for over three minutes) that I didn't know what to do.'

Thomas Alva Edison exhibits his phonograph at Crystal Palace. The former Prime Minister, William Ewart Gladstone, and two poets, Browning and Tennyson, set their voices in wax.

1889   28 May: Returning from honeymoon, Edward Elgar settles in Kensington but makes no mark on the musical scene.
7 December: Amid a bitter quarrel, Gilbert and Sullivan produce *The Gondoliers*.

1891   31 January: Carte opens an English Opera House with Sullivan's *Ivanhoe*, which runs for 155 performances.

1892   June: Gustav Mahler conducts London's second *Ring* cycle, as well as *Tristan*, *Tannhäuser* and *Fidelio*, in imported Hamburg productions at Covent Garden.

1893   29 May: Deeply depressed, Tchaikovsky arrives to conduct his 4th symphony and collect a doctorate from Cambridge. 'I suffer not only from torments which cannot be put into words – there is one place in my new Symphony, the Sixth, where they seem to me adequately expressed – but from a dislike of strangers and an indefinable terror – though of what the devil alone knows,' he writes home.
2 December: Queen's Hall (QH) opens at the top of Regent Street with a performance of Mendelssohn's 2nd symphony in an admirable acoustic.

1894   14 May: Puccini attends local première of *Manon Lescaut*.
30 October: The composer-critic Philip Heseltine (pseud. Peter Warlock) is born at the Savoy Hotel.

1895   10 August: Henry Wood, aged 26, conducts the first Promenade Concert at Queen's Hall, inaugurating a summer tradition. The opening programme contains 22 items.

1896   7 March: *The Grand Duke* is Gilbert and Sullivan's last gasp.
19 March: Dvořák hears his cello concerto premièred by Leo Stern.
10 December: An all-Fauré concert is attended by the composer.

1897   7 December: Richard Strauss makes his first appearance.

1898   May: The Gramophone Company sets up at 31 Maiden

Lane, near the Strand, initially as an outlet for US products. It builds a pressing factory and subsidiary at Hanover, called Deutsche Grammophon Gesellschaft.

July: Fred Gaisberg arrives from the US and sets up a studio at Maiden Lane. He becomes the first record producer.

21 June: Gabriel Fauré conducts incidental music for Mrs Patrick Campbell's performance of Maeterlinck's play *Pelléas et Mélisande* at the Prince of Wales Theatre.

1899   19 April: Sergei Rachmaninov, 26, makes his London début. He appears regularly for the next 40 years.

The Gramophone Company purchases a canine painting by Francis Barraud, 'His Master's Voice', as its trademark.

30 May: Frederick Delius's first concert of his own music fails miserably at St James's Hall.

19 June: Hans Richter's performance there of Elgar's Variations on an Original Theme (Enigma) marks the dawn of an English musical renaissance.

1900   28 May: The death of George Grove.

22 November: His friend Arthur Sullivan dies; these deaths end the Victorian era in music. The old Queen dies the following year.

1901   30 May: *Much Ado About Nothing*, Charles Villiers Stanford's Shakespearean opera, folds after two nights at Covent Garden; Vaughan Williams considers it 'a splendid work with all the certainty of popularity'.

31 May: 'The most perfect concert hall in London', built by the Bechstein piano company in Wigmore Street, opens with a star recital by Ferruccio Busoni and Eugène Ysaÿe. It survives as the Wigmore Hall.

20 July: Elgar presents his overture *Cockaigne (In London Town)*, 'to my friends, the members of British orchestras'.

1902   18 March: Fred Gaisberg goes to Milan to make the first credible vocal recording. Enrico Caruso, 30, makes his Covent Garden début in May as a record star.

1904   27 May: Joachim celebrates 60 years of London concerts with a performance of the Beethoven concerto with his own cadenza. His portrait is painted by John Singer Sargent.

9 June: The London Symphony Orchestra (LSO), a band of rebels from Henry Wood's Queen's Hall, gives its opening concert with Hans Richter as conductor.

The Aeolian Hall opens on Bond Street.

1905　2 January: Michael Tippett is born at Eastcote.

8 March: Elgar conducts the LSO in his *Introduction and Allegro for String*, Op. 47.

St James's Hall is demolished.

21 October: For the centenary of Nelson's victory over the French fleet at Trafalgar, Henry Wood performs his own Fantasia on British Sea-Songs. It becomes a Proms perennial.

December: Thomas Beecham, 26, debuts with a band of 40 Queen's Hall men and a baritone at the Bechstein Hall in eighteenth-century French and Italian pieces and a ballad by Cyril Scott. 'The conductor suffered,' reports *The Times*, 'from what was practically insubordination on the part of the players.'

1906　January: The London Symphony Orchestra pays its maiden visit to Paris, performing at the Châtelet under the batons of Stanford, Edouard Colonne and André Messager.

1 July: Manuel Garcia, inventor of the laryngoscope and influential singing teacher, dies aged 106. He was the son of Rossini's first Almaviva and brother of the legendary mezzos, Maria Malibran and Pauline Viardot.

1 December: Adelina Patti bids her final farewell.

1907　HMV builds a factory and recording studio at Hayes, on London's western outskirts.

1908　1 February: Debussy, conducting *La Mer*, earns greater applause than at home, though *The Times* finds it 'obvious that he renounces melody as definitely as Alberich renounces love'. Ralph Vaughan Williams, 36, goes to Paris to study with Maurice Ravel.

1909　22 February: Beecham introduces the Beecham Symphony Orchestra in the Berlioz *Te Deum*.

7 June: He premières Frederick Delius's *Mass of Life*, an irreligious setting of Nietzschean ideas (QH).

9 June: Stanford performs an *Ode to Discord* in protest at the orchestrations of Strauss and Debussy:

Philatelic tributes to musical masterpieces.

Hence, loathed Melody!
Divine Cacophony assume
The rightful overlordship in her room
And with Percussion's stimulating aid,
Expel the Heavenly but no longer youthful Maid!

1910   19 February: Backed by his wealthy father, Beecham opens an operatic season at Covent Garden with the UK première of Strauss's *Elektra*. Other local novelties include Ethel Smyth's *The Wreckers* and Delius's *Village Romeo and Juliet*. Richard Strauss and Bruno Walter are among his guest-conductors.
10 November: Fritz Kreisler premières Elgar's violin concerto (QH).

8 December: Beecham introduces a *Salome* from which many biblical references have been excised on government order but are restored by subversive singers.

1911   24 May: Elgar conducts his 2nd symphony, dedicated to 'His Late Majesty King Edward VII'.

29 May: Leaping into his garden pond at Harrow Weald to rescue a drowning girl, W. S. Gilbert, 74, suffers a heart attack and dies with a chivalrous smile.

Solomon Cutner, an 8-year-old pianist, makes his début in Tchaikovsky's 1st concerto.

1912   28 March: The LSO departs for a triumphant inaugural tour of North America, switching its booking at the last moment to avoid the ill-fated *Titanic*. Returning in May, it records several overtures at Hayes with Arthur Nikisch.

The composer Ethel Smyth is imprisoned in Holloway Gaol for throwing bricks through the Home Secretary's window in support of universal suffrage for women.

3 September: Schoenberg's 'Five Pieces for Orchestra', Op. 16, are presented at the Proms by Sir Henry Wood, who tells his players, 'Stick to it, gentlemen. This is nothing to what you'll have to play in twenty-five years' time!'

24 September: Wood performs Frank Bridge's evocative suite, *The Sea*.

1913   24 June: Beecham brings the Diaghilev company to Drury Lane for a Grand Season of opera and ballet, including Stravinsky's *Le Sacre du Printemps* fresh from its Paris riot.

18 October: Women play for the first time in a professional London orchestra – six join Wood's Queen's Hall band.

1914   13 March: Preparing for a Proms concert on his only UK visit, Alexander Skryabin contracts a fatal lip infection.

27 March: A London Symphony by Vaughan Williams is performed in its original version: he revises it six years later.

[4 August: Britain declares war on Germany.]

1915   6 July: Elgar conducts *Polonia* for Polish war victims, dedicated to Ignacy Jan Paderewski.

October: The Beecham Opera Company opens with pieces by Smyth and Stanford.

1916   5 August: George Butterworth, gifted composer and *The Times*'s music critic, is killed on the Somme.

1917   20 February: A concert by Heseltine, Cecil Gray and Bernard van Dieren at the Wigmore (formerly Bechstein) Hall is critically abused because of the composers' alleged pacifist and pro-German sentiments.

1918   29 September: Given the QH orchestra for a morning by the wealthy composer Balfour Gardiner, Gustav Holst gets Adrian Boult to conduct the private première of his suite, The Planets, for an audience of friends and pupils.
[11 November: Armistice ends the First World War.]

1919   21 May: Elgar's string quartet in E minor, Op. 83, is given at Wigmore Hall.
27 October: His cello concerto, mourning the world lost at war and his wife newly dead, is played by Felix Salmond under the composer's baton.

1920   February: A public broadcasting station is started by the Marconi Company at Chelmsford.
27 April: Stravinsky's *Ragtime* for 11 instruments is conducted by Arthur Bliss.
14 May: The revised version of Vaughan Williams's London Symphony is conducted by Albert Coates.
11 November: The Armistice Day service at Westminster Abbey is recorded by electrical process – the first such attempt – by two British researchers, Lionel Guest and H. O. Merriman. The sound is relayed by telephone lines to their machine in a building nearby.
December: The Beecham Opera Company goes bankrupt; its members re-group as the British National Opera Company.

1921   10 June: Stravinsky's Symphonies of Wind Instruments, composed in memory of Debussy, is premièred by Serge Koussevitsky.
2 November: Tchaikovsky's *Swan Lake* is danced for the first time in western Europe at the Alhambra Theatre by the Diaghilev company.
26 November: Karol Szymanowski's 3rd symphony, 'Song of the Night', intended for St Petersburg but overtaken by revolution, is conducted on the cheap by the Russian-born Albert Coates, substituting organ and cello for chorus and tenor.

1922   24 January: William Walton's *Façade* is privately premièred.

26 January: Vaughan Williams's Pastoral Symphony, his 3rd, is conducted by Boult.

The British Broadcasting Company starts operations from Savoy Hill on the 2LO station.

1923　8 January: The first opera broadcast – *The Magic Flute* from Covent Garden.

3 April: George Gershwin presents *The Rainbow*, featuring the songs 'Sunday in London Town' and 'Moonlight in Versailles'.

24 March: Béla Bartók at the Aeolian Hall gives the UK première of his first violin sonata with its dedicatee, Jelly d'Aranyi.

7 May: With the same partner, he plays his second sonata. He returns to Budapest carrying a huge bunch of bananas, of which he has become inordinately fond.

The novelist Compton Mackenzie founds a monthly magazine, *The Gramophone*, to campaign for improved disc quality. Electrical recording is about to arrive.

1924　17 March: Stanford, 71, suffers a stroke on St Patrick's Day, dies 12 days later and is buried in Westminster Abbey.

26 April: Ravel accompanies Jelly d'Aranyi to première *Tzigane*.

4 July: Vaughan Williams's opera, *Hugh the Drover*, is staged at the Royal College of Music.

21 July: For the opening of Wembley Stadium and the British Empire Exhibition, Elgar offers an *Empire March*.

Electrical innovations.

131

8 September: George Gershwin introduces *Primrose*, a brand-new musical, at the Winter Garden. It runs for 255 nights but never reaches New York.

1926   28 April: Leoš Janáček, 71, the first Czech composer to visit since Dvořák, is stranded by the General Strike.
8 June: Melba's farewell at Covent Garden.
3 December: Lord Berners's ballet *The Triumph of Neptune* danced by Diaghilev's troupe at the Lyceum.

1927   May: The BBC rescues the debt-ridden Proms, slashing the sentimental ballads but retaining Wood as principal conductor. It is the new Corporation's first involvement in concert activity.

1929   The Decca Gramophone company is founded by an industrialist, Edward Lewis.
21 March: Vaughan Williams's opera *Sir John in Love* at the RCM.
15 July: Diaghilev presents a 16-year-old protégé, Igor Markevitch, playing his own piano concerto at Covent Garden.
Thursday night at the Proms is reserved for British composers.
3 October: Paul Hindemith is soloist in Walton's viola concerto after Lionel Tertis, the intended performer, rejects the score.
12 October: Beecham stages a Delius Festival in the presence of the ailing composer.
4 November: Yehudi Menuhin, 13, makes an historic London début in the Brahms concerto, and soon elects to settle here.

1930   1 January: Adrian Boult, 40, is named music director of the BBC.
22 October: He conducts its new Symphony Orchestra in an opening concert of Wagner, Brahms, Saint-Saëns and Ravel (QH).
17 December: Philip Heseltine, 36, critic who composed under the pseudonym Peter Warlock, commits suicide. He is depicted in Antony Powell's *A Dance to the Music of Time*.

1931   6 January: A restored music hall in Islington is the home of the new Sadler's Wells (SW) opera, ballet and theatre companies.
March: HMV and UK Columbia merge to form Electrical and Music Industries – EMI.

11 November: They open a recording studio at Abbey Road, St John's Wood.

1932   Artur Schnabel records all 32 Beethoven sonatas for HMV.
7 October: Beecham launches the London Philharmonic Orchestra (LPO).

1933   After Hitler's rise to power, a wave of musicians seeks refuge in London.
EMI tries stereo recording, but shelves it.

1934   This year sees the deaths of:
23 February: Elgar (aged 76)
25 May: Holst (59)
10 June: Delius (72).
May: A summer opera festival is opened at a private country house in Glyndebourne, Sussex.
27 September: Vaughan Williams conducts the BBC Symphony Orchestra in Fantasia on Greensleeves, lifted from his opera *Sir John in Love*.
3 December: Impatient for Walton to finish his first symphony, the BBC performs three extant movements.

1935   10 April: Boult gives Vaughan Williams's dissonant 4th symphony.
28 June: At the end of a 6-month sojourn in Earls Court, German refugee Kurt Weill stages *A Kingdom for a Cow*, an instant failure. He moves on to America.

1936   3 May: Anton Webern conducts the BBC Symphony Orchestra in the last concert of his life. He returns to Vienna where his services are not required.
A Londoner, John Barbirolli, 37, is picked by the New York Philharmonic to succeed Arturo Toscanini.
November: Beecham tours Nazi Germany with the London Philharmonic. In a breathtaking fire, Crystal Palace is demolished.

1937   30 April: 1st symphony by Edmund Rubbra.
9 May: After the traumatic abdication of his brother, Edward VIII, George VI's coronation is enlivened by Walton's *Crown Imperial* march.
June: An opera is experimentally televised – Act 3 of Gounod's *Faust* from Alexandra Palace.
27 August: Benjamin Britten's Variations on a Theme of Frank

Bridge earn acclaim at Salzburg.

1938   17 June: The highlight of the London festival of the International Society for Contemporary Music is the world première of Webern's *Das Augenlicht*, with Hermann Scherchen conducting the BBC Symphony Orchestra.
18 August: Britten, 24, plays his own piano concerto.
7 September: He conducts the Bridge Variations at the Proms.
20 October: *The Serf*, second opera by George Lloyd, 25, is mangled at Covent Garden by Albert Coates.

1939   [1 September: Outbreak of the Second World War.]
Beecham liquidates the London Philharmonic and prepares to depart for the US and Australia. The orchestra, refusing to die, becomes a self-governing band beneath a monogram designed by Sir Edwin Lutyens and a Manifesto written by J. B. Priestley.
10 October: In the evacuated National Gallery, pianist Myra Hess inaugurates lunchtime recitals that continue throughout the war; during the Blitz she plays in the basement.

1940   21 April: Michael Tippett conducts the South London Orchestra, an *ad hoc* body of unemployed musicians, in his first masterpiece, the Concerto for double string orchestra, at Morley College, where he teaches. When the college is destroyed by a mine, he discovers Purcell scores in the rubble of its library.

1941   10 May: Queen's Hall is flattened by German bombs.
Having virtually ceased to compose, Sir Arnold Bax is named Master of the Queen's Musick.

1942   17 April: Britten and Pears return from America, register as conscientious objectors and are required to give musical service instead of military.

1943   21 June: Tippett is jailed at Wormwood Scrubs for three months for refusing socially useful work in exchange for conscientious exemption from military service. Vaughan Williams testifies vainly on his behalf; Britten and Pears visit him in jail; he takes over the small prison orchestra from Ivor Novello, convicted of fiddling petrol coupons.
25 June: Vaughan Williams conducts his serene 5th symphony at the Proms.
23 August: Tippett goes straight from jail to a performance of his second string quartet at the Wigmore Hall.
28 September: *Freedom Morning*, based on Negro spirituals, by

serving US airman Marc Blitzstein, is performed by the LSO with a 200-strong chorus of black servicemen.

15 October: Britten's *Serenade for Tenor, Horn and Strings* is conducted by Walter Goehr, with Pears and Dennis Brain as soloists.

1944   19 March: Tippett's oratorio, *A Child of our Time*, inspired by the 1938 shooting of a German diplomat by a young Jewish refugee and liberally woven with Negro spirituals, is performed by Goehr, conducting the LPO and various choirs at the Adelphi Theatre.

19 August: Three weeks after his last Prom, Sir Henry Wood dies.

1945   [7 May: War ends in Europe.]

7 June: Britten's *Peter Grimes* at Sadler's Wells – England's first operatic masterpiece since Purcell's *Dido*, 255 years earlier – revives the indigenous art of opera.

27 October: The Philharmonia, formed by EMI producer Walter Legge, gives its first public concert: Beecham conducts Mozart.

1946   The Arts Council of Great Britain is created to distribute state subsidy to the arts. Rebuffed by the LPO and the Philharmonia, Beecham founds the Royal Philharmonic (RPO), London's fifth orchestra; Britten and friends start the English Opera Group.

7 July: The International Society for Contemporary Music reassembles in London with Prokofiev's *Ode to the End of the War*.

12 July: Webern's first cantata (Op. 29) is conducted by Karl Rankl.

12 July: Kathleen Ferrier, 34, makes her operatic début as the victim in Britten's *Rape of Lucretia* (Glyndebourne).

29 September: The BBC opens a Third Programme devoted to serious music and speech.

October: Richard Strauss returns to London to conduct three orchestras and regain political acceptability.

1947   20 June: Britten's *Albert Herring* is staged at Glyndebourne.

1948   22 March: The musical-maker Andrew Lloyd Webber is born at Westminster Hospital.

11 April: Herbert von Karajan makes his London début, conducting Dinu Lipatti in the Schumann concerto.

21 April: Boult and the RPO give Vaughan Williams's 6th symphony.

24 October: Francis Poulenc's *Sinfonietta*, his only original concert piece for orchestra alone, is premièred by the BBC.

15 November: Tippett's *A Birthday Suite for Prince Charles* is performed by the BBC to celebrate the royal birth.

1949   26 January: Rubbra's 5th symphony, written during his conversion to Roman Catholicism, is performed by Boult.

1950   22 May: Richard Strauss's 'Four Last Songs' are premièred posthumously by Kirsten Flagstad, with Furtwängler conducting (RAH).

1951   The Royal Festival Hall (RFH) opens as the centrepiece of the Festival of Britain.

21 August: Death of Constant Lambert, 45.

13 November: Nikolai Medtner, 71, exiled Russian composer, dies.

1 December: Britten conducts *Billy Budd* at Covent Garden.

1953   8 June: Britten's *Gloriana* marks the coronation of Elizabeth II.

8 October: Cancer claims Kathleen Ferrier, 41.

Sir Arthur Bliss becomes Master of the Queen's Musick on Bax's death.

1954   1 February: Boult broadcasts 8th symphony by Havergal Brian, a 78-year-old composer unheard in London for 40 years. Its success prompts him to write a further 26 symphonies.

13 June: Vaughan Williams provides a concerto for tuba.

13 July: Leading Polish composer Andrzej Panufnik defects in Switzerland and makes a new life in London.

Four British operas are premièred in a single season:

22 September: Lennox Berkeley's *Nelson* (SW)

6 October: Britten's *Turn of the Screw* (SW) (World première, Venice, 14 September 1954)

3 December: Walton's *Troilus and Cressida* (ROH) and, most strikingly:

1955 27 January: Tippett's *The Midsummer Marriage*, with Joan Sutherland in the role of Jenifer.

1956 The Royal Ballet is constituted.

1957 1 September: Dennis Brain, 36, horn player, smashes his car into a Hertfordshire tree.

1958 5 February: Boult's live broadcast première of Tippett's 2nd symphony breaks down after a few bars.
2 April: After two rehearsals, one of them paid for by the composer, Sir Malcolm Sargent conducts the RPO in Vaughan Williams's 9th symphony.
26 August: Preparing to attend the recording of his symphony, Ralph Vaughan Williams, 86, dies at home in Camden Town.

1959 17 February: Joan Sutherland attains stardom with sensational *Lucia* at Covent Garden.
7 July: Ernest Newman, outstanding Wagner biographer and *Sunday Times* critic, dies aged 90.

1960 17 June: Harrison Birtwistle's music is heard in town: *Monody for Corpus Christi* is conducted by John Carewe at the smallest South Bank hall.
6 September: Shostakovich introduces Britten in London to his cellist friend Mstislav Rostropovich, inaugurating a creative trialogue.
13 August: Mahler's 10th symphony is played in a provisional performing version by a BBC producer, Deryck Cooke. It is soon banned by the composer's widow, Alma.

Vaughan Williams – the grand old man of English music.

Ralph Vaughan Williams 1872/1958

9p

11 October: The English Chamber Orchestra comes into being.

1961   8 February: Roberto Gerhard's abstract *Collages* performed.
8 March: Death of Beecham, 81.
October: Georg Solti becomes music director at Covent Garden
for the next decade.

1962   21 February: Nureyev and Fonteyn come together at
Covent Garden.
Launch of Faber Music, an independent publisher created by
Britten and the critic Donald Mitchell.

1963   2 July: *Our Man in Havana*, an opera by Australian composer Malcolm Williamson after Graham Greene's novel, is
staged at Sadler's Wells.

1964   26 May: Aaron Copland conducts the LSO in *Music for a
Great City*, commissioned by the orchestra for its 60th anni-
versary – but depicting New York, not London.
13 August: Cooke's revised version of Mahler's 10th symphony

Britten plays duets with Rostropovich.

is conducted by Berthold Goldschmidt (RAH).

1966   Dr Ray Dolby's London laboratories invent the Dolby System that removes the background hiss from music tapes.

1967   1 March: Queen Elizabeth Hall (QEH), the second South Bank auditorium, opens with a concert conducted by Britten, amid an architectural mess of concrete walkways.
30 May: The Fires of London, an instrumental group formed by Birtwistle and Maxwell Davies to play their modernities, gives inaugural concert at QEH.
The Beatles record their *Abbey Road* album.

1968   24 January: Enter the London Sinfonietta, an up-to-the-minute new music orchestra.
21 August: Sadler's Wells Opera moves to the Coliseum and (in 1974) takes the name English National Opera (ENO).

1969   14 February: Hans Werner Henze conducts *Essay on Pigs*, a reflection on police-student relations in Berlin.
19 February: Sinfonietta play Birtwistle's *Verses for Ensembles*.
22 April: *Eight Songs for a Mad King*, a gruesome view of George III's insanity with excerpts from Handel to the Beatles, is Maxwell Davies's contribution to music drama (QEH).
19 May: Britten's *Children's Crusade* cantata is sung at St Paul's Cathedral.

1970   Pierre Boulez is named principal conductor of the BBC Symphony Orchestra, inaugurating an era of new music, late-night talk-in concerts and mixed-media events.
24 May: Panufnik's *Universal Prayer* is performed by Leopold Stokowski in a New York cathedral and repeated by him days later at Twickenham parish church.
14 October: Rostropovich performs Witold Lutosławski's cello concerto (RFH).
20 November: In *Nenia: the death of Orpheus*, Birtwistle discovers an obsessive theme; it is performed at the BBC studios, Maida Vale.
2 December: Covent Garden sees its first topless female soloist in Tippett's multi-layered *The Knot Garden*.

1971   June: The International Society of Contemporary Music's 45th festival presents music by some 40 composers.
October: The rock opera *Jesus Christ Superstar*, by Andrew Lloyd Webber and Tim Rice, is mounted in London and New York.

Colin Davis takes over as music director at the ROH.
26 November: The Prime Minister, Edward Heath, conducts the LSO in Elgar's *Cockaigne*.

1972 22 June: Tippett's 3rd symphony, modelled on Mahler's *Das Lied von der Erde*, is performed by Colin Davis and the LSO with Heather Harper as soloist (RFH).
12 July: *Taverner* by Peter Maxwell Davies, a fantasy on the torments of the Tudor composer, is staged at the ROH.
18 July: Menuhin plays Panufnik's violin concerto at the Guildhall.
24 August: At the Proms, Cornelius Cardew's Scratch Orchestra delivers *The Great Learning*, a musical distillation of Mao Zedong's revolutionary doctrines.
8 December: Riccardo Muti, 31, becomes principal conductor of the New Philharmonia Orchestra.

1973 17 April: *Infidelio*, Elisabeth Lutyens's chamber opera, is staged.
7 May: Britten undergoes unsuccessful open-heart surgery at the National Heart Hospital, forcing him to miss, on 16 June, *Death in Venice*, his last opera, at Aldeburgh.

1974 Birtwistle is named music director of the new National Theatre, where he composes for productions as diverse as *The Oresteia* and *Amadeus*.
20 October: Henze's *Tristan* and Elliott Carter's *Brass Quintet* are premièred on the same day in separate concerts.

1975 27 March: Death of Sir Arthur Bliss, 83, leads to the appointment of Malcolm Williamson as Master of the Queen's Musick.
2 April: Boulez conducts his *Rituel in memoriam Bruno Maderna.*

1976 12 June: Britten is the first composer elevated to the House of Lords. He dies six months later.
12 July: Henze's Marxist opera *We Come to the River* flops at Covent Garden.

1977 2 February: Peter Shaffer's play *The Royal Hunt of the Sun* transfers to ENO as an opera by Iain Hamilton.
1 July: Playwright Tom Stoppard collaborates with André Previn in *Every Good Boy Deserves Favour*, a musical satire on abuses in Soviet psychiatric hospitals, performed at the RFH. The initials form music's best-known mnemonic.

6 July: Birtwistle's *Bow Down* is staged at the National Theatre.
7 July: Lasers criss-cross the ROH in Tippett's *The Ice Break*.

1978   2 February: Simon Rattle, 23, conducts and records Maxwell Davies's hour-long 1st symphony with the Philharmonia.
21 June: Lloyd Webber's *Evita* opens in the West End.
15 July: His Variations on a Theme of Paganini are played by his
cellist brother Julian, and a rock band at the RFH.

1979   February: Decca announces the dawn of digital recording.
6 September: Oliver Knussen, 27, conducts his 15-minute 3rd
symphony.
2 November: Peter Shaffer's play *Amadeus*, a popular fiction on

Simon Rattle.

the rivalry between Mozart and Salieri, opens at the National Theatre.

1980 23 April: 2nd symphony by the Soviet composer Alfred Schnittke, unperformable in the USSR, is premièred by Gennady Rozhdestvensky.
June–July: Musicians call a 2-month national strike against the BBC over its plan to disband three orchestras; the Proms are postponed.
22 August: Tippett's triple concerto, one of his most engaging works, is directed by Sir Colin Davis at the Proms.
25 August: George Benjamin, 20, is the youngest composer to receive a Prom première, with *Ringed by the Flat Horizon*.

1981 19 February: The 20-volume *New Grove Dictionary of Music and Musicians* reforms the musical reference work.
15 April: Julian Lloyd Webber plays a cello concerto commissioned from the blind Spanish composer, Joaquín Rodrigo.
11 May: His brother Andrew scores a further West End hit with *Cats*, based on T. S. Eliot's least serious poetry.

1982 3 March: The £153 million Barbican Centre provides a home for the LSO, Guildhall School of Music and Royal Shakespeare Company, but is criticized for rambling design and muffled acoustics.
26 October: Elliott Carter's *In Sleep, In Thunder* is played by the Sinfonietta.

1983 Deaths of:
22 February: Sir Adrian Boult, 93
8 March: Sir William Walton, 81
14 April: Elisabeth Lutyens, 76.

1984 9 January: Knussen's children's fantasy *Where the Wild Things Are* is staged in its final version.
18 October: The Sinfonietta introduces Birtwistle's landmark work *Secret Theatre*.

1985 13 July: Live Aid, a rock fund-raiser for African drought at Wembley Stadium, is watched globally by some 1,500 million people.
3 December: York Höller's piano concerto, played by Peter

Donohoe (RFH), is the BBC's commission for European Music Year.

1986   21 May: Birtwistle's *Mask of Orpheus*, 15 years in the making, attracts worldwide attention after six sell-out shows at ENO. Budget cuts prevent its revival.
5 August: *Yan Tan Tethera*, Birtwistle's second opera this year, is staged at the South Bank.
29 October: *The Man who Mistook his Wife for a Hat*, a minimalist opera by Michael Nyman based on a neurological case-history, is staged at the ICA.
10 November: Elena Firsova's haunting *Earthly Life* is introduced by the Nash Ensemble (QEH).
Sir Colin Davis leaves Covent Garden, Bernard Haitink arrives.

1987   20 January: The Fires of London break up after two Maxwell Davies premières at its 20th birthday concert (QEH).
25 February: Panufnik conducts his 9th symphony (RFH).
25 August: Throat cancer forces Klaus Tennstedt to leave the LPO; Claudio Abbado quits the LSO for the Vienna State Opera.
19 October: Tragic death from multiple sclerosis of cellist Jacqueline du Pré, 42.

1988   17 April: Berthold Goldschmidt, 85, attends the première of *Beatrice Cenci*, an opera that won him the Festival of Britain prize almost 40 years before (QEH).
29 April: The first woman to conduct at Covent Garden, Sian Edwards, 29, directs Tippett's *The Knot Garden*.
5 June: A lost Donizetti opera, *Elisabeth*, is discovered in the vaults of the Royal Opera House.
Autumn: The complete works of Schoenberg and symphonies of Shostakovich are performed concurrently in London, a twentieth-century survey unparalleled in any other city.

1989   18 March: Elena Firsova's Chamber Concerto No. 4 is played by the Sinfonietta.
28 April: Benedict Mason's *Lighthouse of England and Wales* is performed by the BBC.
23 May: David Blake's opera, *The Plumber's Gift*, attacks the greed and selfishness of the Thatcher era (ENO).

1989   23 June: The Belgian Henri Pousseur presents *Mnémosyne*

Jacqueline du Pré, lamented cellist.

doublement obstinée on his 60th birthday.

28 June: John Casken's opera *Golem*, on the Prague Jewish legend, is staged at the Almeida.

31 October: György Kurtág's *Requiem for a Friend* premières at a wide-ranging Hungarian Festival at the Barbican.

1990   18 May: ENO stages Robin Holloway's opera on the longest

Sian Edwards – a bold, egalitarian choice at the English National Opera.

novel in the English language, Samuel Richardson's *Clarissa*.
September: The London Philharmonic become resident orchestra at the South Bank under a 30-year-old Austrian conductor, Franz Welser-Möst.

1991 30 May: Birtwistle's opera on the Arthurian legend of *Gawain and the Green Knight* opens at Covent Garden.

1992 Sian Edwards appointed music director at ENO.
17 March: ENO is given £12.8 million by the government and independent arts foundation to buy the Coliseum and secure its future.
25 June: Andrzej Panufnik's cello concerto receives posthumous première by Rostropovich and the LSO.

PART THREE

7

A CONSUMER'S GUIDE TO MUSICAL LONDON

The nightly array of London's musical riches is often so profuse that the listener faces an agonizing choice: not where to go, but what you can afford to miss.

On the same evening you might find Carlo Maria Giulini or Ricardo Muti conducting Mozart at the Royal Festival Hall while Mstislav Rostropovich plays Prokofiev at the Barbican. Placido Domingo is singing at Covent Garden, while the English National Opera is reviving one of its Janáček triumphs. At the smaller South Bank auditoria, the London Sinfonietta is trawling choppy contemporary waters, while at the Wigmore Hall a young American quartet is midway through a Shostakovich cycle. Family favourites are on parade at Fairfields Hall, Glydebourne is in full swing, there is an oddball chamber opera at the Almeida, a live Berlin Philharmonic relay on Radio 3 and heaven alone knows what is on at the music colleges.

Where on earth to begin?
With the morning newspapers. Four of the serious dailies, *The Times*, *Guardian*, *Daily Telegraph* and *Independent*, carry substantial listings of cultural events; the Saturday editions and the *Sunday Times*, *Observer* and *Independent on Sunday* issue weekly recommendations. From time to time, national newspapers offer special discounts on concert and opera bookings.

The weeklies *Time Out*, *City Limits* and *What's on in London* run classical music diaries, though less committedly than their rock coverage. *Classical Music*, a fortnightly magazine, features detailed advertisements from the major halls, as well as news and gossip from around the music world. The desks in concert-hall foyers are littered with brochures for forthcoming events. Take home a fistful to peruse in the smallest room.

How to choose
Study the lists and select the most interesting works and artists. If the performers seem unfamiliar, check the promoter's name at the foot of the announcement. If it is not the orchestra (e.g. LSO Ltd) or the hall itself (e.g. South Bank Board) that is putting on the concert, beware. Commercial impresarios stage many concerts at the major halls with untried artists and short rehearsals. The musical quality of many of these promotions is dubious, even when the orchestra is a reputable one. When in doubt about a concert, pick a known soloist or promoter.

If the event of your choice is sold out, you can try queuing for returns on the night, but this is as chancy as going on standby for a flight to Ouagadougou. The ensuing disappointment is disproportional to the original ambition.

For a last-minute concert urge, wander down to the South Bank, where you are bound to find a spare seat in one of the three halls. West End visitors will find it worth dropping in on the off-chance to the enchanting Wigmore Hall. Bear in mind that most concerts start at 7.30 or 7.45 p.m. and finish around 9.30 p.m.

Concerts are given nightly (except 24, 25 December and 1 January) at:

	average prices	tel.*
Barbican Hall, EC2 (principally orchestral)	£4–28	071-638 8891
Royal Festival Hall, SE1 (orchestral and occasional star recitals)	£5–25	071-928 8800 (bookings) 071-928 3002 (enquiries)
Queen Elizabeth Hall, SE1 (small orchestras and chamber music)	£5–15	as RFH
Purcell Room, SE1 (chamber and instrumental)	£5–10	as RFH
Wigmore Hall, W1 (chamber music, closed July–August)	£4–15	071-935 2141

* When telephoning within London, the prefix 071/081 need only be added when dialling from outside the respective area.

Regular concerts can also be found at:

St John's Smith Square, SW1	£5–15	071-222 1061
Royal Albert Hall, SW7	£9–27	071-589 8212

Occasional/seasonal performances are given at:

Almeida Theatre, Almeida Street, Islington, N1	071-359 4404
Conway Hall, Red Lion Square, WC1 (Sunday night chamber music, October –April)	071-242 8032
Institute of Contemporary Arts (ICA), The Mall, SW1	071-930 6393/ 3647
New Gallery Centre, 123 Regent Street, W1	071-734 8888
St Martin-in-the-Fields Church, Trafalgar Square, WC2	071-839 1930

Enjoying the Proms is an art in its own right. The season runs at the Royal Albert Hall from the third week of July to the middle of September and is rendered coherent and plannable by a BBC booklet published in early May at around £3, available at most bookshops and station bookstalls. The cost of this guide can be instantly recouped by using coupons that it provides for discounted tickets to esoteric and late-night concerts.

You can book by mail from May (Proms Concerts, Royal Albert Hall, SW7 2AP) or by phone (071-823 9998) from the beginning of June. Tickets run from £3.50 to £42, but standing seats start at £2 and admission to the entire season can be purchased for as little as £70, probably the best musical bargain anywhere this side of the celestial heights. A season ticket also procures automatic right of admission to the Last Night, which is more of a religio-national ritual than a musical occasion. Anyone buying more than five seats at a time is entitled to apply for a Last Night ticket–subject, as they say, to availability and the voltage of your smile at the box-office clerk.

It is always advisable to arrive early at the Royal Albert Hall. Several concerts are preceded by pre-Prom talks starting at 6.15 p.m., and you can extend your social life markedly amid the youngsters who mill around the concourse in the sunny hour before the opening chord.

Outside central London
There is a wide range of concert activity taking place outside central London. To the south, in Croydon, Fairfields Hall (tel. 081-688 9291) produces regular events; eastwards, Blackheath Concert Halls (tel. 081-463 0100) provide a lovely setting for increasingly ambitious programmes. North London relies on occasional offerings at venues like the Wembley Conference Centre, while the boom-town Dockland areas have yet to get their cultural act fully together. There is a Docklands Sinfonietta (tel. 071-712 0420) that gives concerts in St Mary's Rotherhithe. Pavarotti has sung at the vast London Arena in Milwall (tel. 071-538 1212) and Shakespeare's old Globe Theatre is busily being restored. By the mid-1990s Docklands could become a cultural centre.

Unadvertised concerts
Concerts of astonishingly high quality are a feature of daily life at the principal music colleges. Call the following for details:

Goldsmiths' College, SE14	081-692 7171
Guildhall School of Music, EC2	071-628 2571
London College of Music, W1	071-437 6120
Morley College, SE1	071-928 8501
Royal Academy of Music, NW1	071-935 5461
Royal College of Music, SW7	071-589 3643
Trinity College of Music, W1	071-935 5773

Lunchtime concerts
Concerts of 50–60 minutes' duration are played daily (1 p.m. approx) at the South Bank, the Barbican and on Mondays at St John's Smith Square, and Mondays and Tuesdays at Southwark Cathedral. The Church of St Martin-in-the-Fields (tel. 071-930 0089) has chamber music on Mondays, Tuesdays and Fridays; St George's, Hanover Square, Handel's parish church (tel. 071-629 0874), on Thursdays; St James's, Piccadilly (tel. 071-734 4511), on Thursdays; and other central churches as the spirit moves them. Glance at the church notice board as you pass by. Most church concerts are free, but you may be approached for a donation. See also organ recitals (p. 157).

Concerts for children
These are given on some Saturday mornings at the South Bank and Barbican Centre.

Sunday morning coffee concerts
Given at the Wigmore Hall (11 a.m.), these are an eminently civilized way to start the week. Sunday afternoon (3 p.m.) usually boasts a full triple-hall programme at the South Bank.

Open-air concerts
Concerts of light orchestral music are a feature of summer weekend evenings at Kenwood House, Hampstead, NW3 (tel. 081-348 6684) and Crystal Palace Concert Bowl, Sydenham, SW19 (tel. 081-778 7148).

   Short seasons of music and opera are staged at the Almeida Theatre, N1 (June–July, tel. 071-359 4404), the Royal Albert Hall, SW7 (BBC Promenade Concerts, July–September) and at various venues in the London Opera Festival (June–July).

Knights at the opera
The Royal Opera House, Covent Garden, WC2, alternates between opera and ballet. Opera is sung by international casts in the original language with simultaneous translation beamed above the stage in electronic sur-titles. As at every star-struck house, the outcome is unpredictable. Backstage tantrums, last-minute cancellations and budget cuts can turn the billboard advertisements into fiction and *Otello* into a *Comedy of Errors*. For the prospect of a fine voice or two, you can pay dearly in cash and nerves. Tickets are fearfully expensive, although there are always 500 tickets at below £30.
Prices: £4–120.
Box-office: tel. 071-240 1066/240 1911.

English National Opera sings in the vernacular with mostly home-grown casts in productions that can be brilliantly imaginative or wilfully provocative, depending on your outlook. The Coliseum is a huge but charming auditorium with an unusually friendly atmosphere and its prices are not exorbitant. If bel canto is your bottom line, you may be better served elsewhere, but few companies in the world give a more convincing account of twentieth-century and undeservedly neglected masterpieces.
Prices: £5–45.

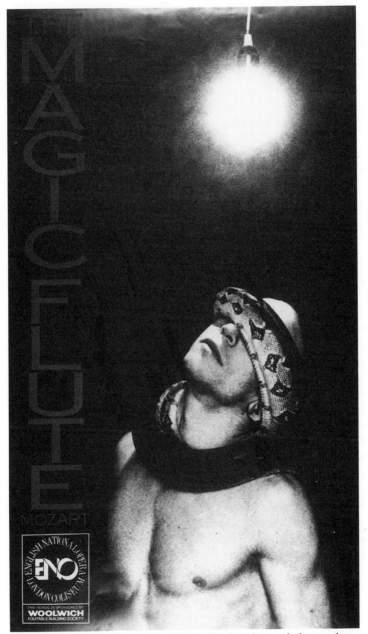

ENO advertised a comely youth with Freudian friend to catch the eye of jaded commuters.

Booking: tel. 071-836 3161 for cash/cheques; 071-240 5258 for credit cards; 071-836 7666 for booking information; 071-836 0111 for general enquiries.

Sadler's Wells in Islington, EC1, houses sporadic middle-brow opera and operettas and imported ballets (tel. 071-278 8916).

The London Opera Festival (June–July, based at Sadler's Wells, tel. 071-837 4878) mounts intriguing chamber operas in fringe West End theatres, alongside the regular fare at Covent Garden and the Coliseum.

Semi-staged operas find their way periodically to the South Bank and crop up in the Almeida Festival. The Royal College of Music gives student productions in its intimate Britten Theatre.

Glyndebourne, an hour's train ride from Victoria or 2½ hours by car on the A23, has its season from May to August and sells almost all seats in advance to subscribers and sponsors. It is unashamedly élitist in artistic standards and entirely unsupported by public subsidy. To experience a well-rehearsed resident company and world-class orchestras (the London Philharmonic and Orchestra of the Age of Enlightenment) in a small house in the heart of England's greenest and most pleasant land is as close to paradise as most of us will come. Get there if you can, and to hell with the cost; evening dress is advisable for ladies, black tie for gents. Bring your own picnic hamper and blanket for the 75-minute Long Interval, or you can order dinner in advance at the much-improved Nether and Middle Wallop Restaurants (reservations: tel. 0273-812510).

Call 071-928 5100 for train times from London, Croydon, Gatwick Airport and Brighton. If you want to fly in by helicopter, call 0273-812321 for landing-site information, rates and requirements. Tickets for Glyndebourne can be booked from the box-office, tel. 0273-812321, or through leading London ticket agencies. Do not travel on the off-chance of picking up a spare pair of seats: they are scarcer than dodos. Ticket prices: £35–90.

How to book

For top performers, apply as far ahead as possible. Get on to the mailing list of your favourite orchestra and opera house – call the marketing department – and you will have priority booking from the launch of the season. Box-office sales usually open thirty days in advance.

At Covent Garden and ENO most first-night seats are mopped up by subscribers, and average capacity over the season hovers at around 90 per cent. Tickets can be hard to find. On the other hand, you stand a better chance of obtaining returns on the night.

Avoid queues – use the telephone.

The First Call booking service (tel. 071-240 7200) takes credit-card reservations for opera, the South Bank and the Royal Albert Hall. No discounts are available, however, and a fee of £1.50 upwards is added.

Where to sit

Common sense suggests that the best seats are the most expensive. Not necessarily. Some top-bracket Barbican seats are located in acoustic Black Holes, while at Covent Garden or the Festival Hall you can find yourself surrounded in the plushest stalls by snoring corporate guests whom the sponsors have wined too well.

At the Royal Festival Hall, front stalls seats on Levels 3 and 4 give the best sound and vision at top price. But the choir seats (price code: A), when available, place you virtually within the orchestra with a percussionist's view of the conductor and soloist, at very low cost; the seats are backless and not recommended for the elderly. At the fringe of the main hall (price code: R) is an inexpensive bank of good seats with restricted vision.

At the Barbican it is harder to find a good, inexpensive place. Try section D, near the stage but with partial vision. Avoid the topmost tiers (sections J, K and L).

The smaller South Bank halls are compact enough for all seats to be acceptable. So is the Wigmore Hall, although connoisseurs try for rows AA and BB at the front left and right of the hall (sold only to personal callers).

The Royal Albert Hall projects a sense of occasion all the way up to its uppermost tiers, but the sound is least diffused in the more expensive ringside rows.

St John's Smith Square is a seventeenth-century church gutted during the last war and painstakingly restored. It has a cosy feel and rather cavernous acoustics unless full; try to sit near the front.

The higher you go in Covent Garden's tiered galleries, the greater the audience involvement and the cheaper it gets. The best bargains at the Coliseum are the stage boxes and upper-circle boxes at mid-price. Both houses keep back seats in the rear amphitheatre or balcony for personal callers on the day of performance, sometimes attracting overnight queues.

Getting it cheap

Anyone aged between 14 and 30 can save up to 50 per cent on tickets to many prime events. Call Youth & Music (tel. 071-379 6722), a philanthropic foundation created in 1954 to foster new audiences.

Discounts of more than 20 per cent are available for most events if purchased as part of a seasonal subscription or for a group of 20 or more. Enquire at the booking office.

Unsold tickets are often sold off cheaply just beforehand to card-carrying students, old-age pensioners and the unemployed. Arrangements vary from one hall and performance to the next; call the box-office to ascertain the prospects.

Residents of the City of Westminster can obtain discounts with a ResCard at halls within the borough. Write for details to: ResCard, City of Westminster, PO Box 240, City Hall, Victoria Street, SW1E 6QP.

Disabilities

A handful of seats are reserved for the disabled and their companions at almost every venue, although toilet facilities are not always suitable. Enquire at the box-office.

How to get there

The two opera houses are exceptionally well served by public transport and inadequately by car parking space. Do not take your car unless you want to emerge from the third act to find it wheel-clamped or stolen. Covent Garden, Holborn, Charing Cross and Leicester Square are the nearest Underground stations and buses depart in every direction. If you are worried about getting mugged on late-night trains, take a taxi home – it will probably cost less than your opera tickets.

Waterloo is the South Bank's nearest station, but romantics dismount at Charing Cross or Embankment and cross the river on foot over the iron railway bridge, taking in an illuminated vista that extends from St Paul's to the Palace of Westminster.

The Wigmore Hall is an easy walk from the Oxford Street and Bond Street Underground stations and bus stops; St John's Smith Square is a riverside stroll from Westminster and the Houses of Parliament.

The Royal Albert Hall has High Street, Kensington and South Kensington Underground stations nearby and buses 9, 10 and 52 that stop right outside.

Getting to and from the Barbican by public transport is less fraught than it used to be, but if the eponymous Underground station is closed there is a bleak 15-minute walk to and from Moorgate or St Paul's. A post-concert bus shuttles to Charing Cross departing fifteen minutes after the end of the concert, but your best bet is to take a taxi or your own car, parking in the ample basement area.

When travelling by road to any weekday evening concert, allow twice as long as you would reasonably think necessary. The traffic in central London jams solid at the slightest accident, demonstration or drop of rain. Set out at six, and you will probably be safe.

Sustaining the spirit

Eating out at the South Bank and Barbican is an unexciting prospect. Each has an average, over-priced restaurant, a dreary fast-food joint and anonymous bars. The trouble is that there are few decent restaurants in the vicinity, and most pull down the shutters at 11 p.m.

At Covent Garden (reservations tel. 071-836 9453) and ENO (tel. 071-836 0111, extn 324) you can pre-order sandwiches and drinks for the intervals, or choose from numerous nearby eating places for a full meal to suit every palate and pocket. Chez Solange (tel. 071-836 0542) is a good French restaurant right on ENO's doorstep, while the lively Bertorelli's (tel. 071-836 3969) is just across the road from the Royal Opera House. The Coliseum is also ringed by cheap-and-cheerful pasta joints and is five minutes' walk from the culinary delights of Chinatown.

If you arrive early at the Barbican, check out the foyer exhibition and what's showing at the Art Gallery. The Royal Festival Hall has a variety of activities in its layered foyers; if you have time, the neighbouring Museum of the Moving Image and the Hayward Gallery are always worth a couple of hours.

The varied restaurants of Marylebone High Street are convenient for the Wigmore Hall, and of Kensington High Street for the Royal Albert Hall.

Where to stay

The more flamboyant musical stars stay at the Savoy, Ritz or Dorchester hotels. Those seeking comfort and privacy often favour Durrant's (George Street, W1, tel. 071-935 8131); the Westbury

(Conduit Street, W1, tel. 071-629 7755) is another common haunt; the Swiss Cottage Holiday Inn (King Henry's Road, NW3, tel. 071-722 7711) is sometimes preferred for its proximity to Abbey Road studios.

Free music
There is a lot of it about, often of remarkably high standard.

The BBC opens its Maida Vale studios from time to time for invitation concerts of esoteric music by its Symphony Orchestra and other groups. (Tel. 071-927 4296 for information.)

Free evening concerts of new music are regularly given at the British Music Information Centre, 10 Stratford Place, W1 (tel. 071-499 8567).

The major music colleges have daytime and evening student

A 1930s' reminder from the Musicians Benevolent Fund.

concerts in wonderfully endowed halls to which the public are welcomed. They occasionally advertise in the music press, or you can call the colleges direct. Student ensembles also play in the foyers of the Barbican and Royal Festival Hall in the early evening.

Organ recitals can be caught at:

St Bride's, Fleet Street, EC4 (1.15, Wednesday), tel. 071-353 1301

St Paul's Cathedral, EC4 (1.15, Friday), tel. 071-248 2705

Southwark Cathedral, SE1 (1.10, Monday), tel. 071-407 3708.

There is brass music in most of the big city parks during the summer, mostly played by military bands. The London Tourist Board (tel. 071-730 3488) publishes details each year.

The British Red Cross and St John's Ambulance Brigade provide volunteer helpers at public performances. If you are medically trained, you will be able to attend outstanding concerts and operas absolutely free – with the obvious risk of having to leave if anyone in the audience faints.

Music to take away

The best places to shop for scores, sheet music and music books are:

Boosey & Hawkes, 295 Regent Street, W1, tel. 071-580 2060

Chappell of Bond Street, 50 New Bond Street, W1, tel. 071-491 2777

Chimes, 44 Marylebone High Street, W1, tel. 071-935 1587

Coliseum Shop, 31 St Martin's Lane, WC2, tel. 071-240 0270

Royal Opera House Shop, James Street, WC2, tel. 071-240 1200

G. Schirmer, 8–9 Frith Street, Soho Square, W1, tel. 071-434 0066

Waterstones in the Royal Festival Hall foyer, SE1, tel. 071-620 0403

Zwemmer's Music Shop, 26 Lichfield Street, Cambridge Circus, WC2, tel. 071-379 7886.

The Barbican Music Shop is hard to find, located outside and to the right of the main entrance. Ignore the small bookstands inside the Barbican, which are miserably stocked for musical purposes.

Rarities and second-hand music find their way to:

H. Baron, Fortune Green, West Hampstead, NW6, tel. 081-459 2035

Decorum Books, 24 Cloudesley Square, Islington, N1, tel. 071-278 1838

Travis & Emery, 17 Cecil Court, Leicester Square, WC2, tel. 071-240 2129.

Chain-operated record stores in every high street purvey the same crop of recent releases. Broader classical selections are stocked at:

Covent Garden Records, 84 Charing Cross Road, WC2, tel. 071-379 7635

HMV Shop, 363 Oxford Street, W1 (next to Bond Street Underground station), tel. 071-629 1240

Music Discount Centre, 29 Rathbone Place, W1 (tel. 071-637 4700); 437 The Strand, WC2; and 1 Creed Lane, Ludgate Hill, near St Paul's, EC4, tel. 071-489 8077

Tower Records, Piccadilly Circus, W1, tel. 071-439 2500.

The Music House, an emporium staffed by dedicated musicians and containing a huge range of records, scores and books, was planned for the King's Road, Chelsea late in 1992.

There are countless makers and retailers of instruments in London, some of international renown – such as J. & A. Beare of Broadwick Street, whose wood-panelled showroom of valuable string instruments is visited by every fiddler of note. Bösendorfer's London Piano Centre, next door to the Wigmore Hall, and Steinway Hall, just around the corner on Marylebone Lane, are subdued places of worship for pianophiles. In principle, seek specialist advice and recommendation before purchasing anything weightier than a tin-whistle. If you want to window-shop, try the third floor of Harrod's department store, or the left-hand side of Charing Cross Road, heading south.

London is the epicentre of world trade in old and valuable instruments. Messrs Beare of Broadwick Street may agree to sell you a Stradivarius for upwards of £400,000, if you can convince them that you are fit to play and preserve it. Pedigree instruments can also be picked up at seasonal auctions at Sotheby's (tel. 071-493 8080), Christie's (tel. 071-839 9060) and Phillips (tel. 071-629 6602).

To buy hi-fi, study trade monthlies like *Hi-Fi News* and *Hi-Fi Choice* at your newsagents for tips, look in the shop windows in Tottenham Court Road, then go to a friendly local dealer, ask for a demonstration of your chosen model and negotiate a price. If anything goes wrong with the equipment, you may be better off buying from a reliable personal retailer than from a chain store.

Music in the air

BBC Radio 3 (90.2–92.4 on the FM band) relays serious music, broken by bursts of even more serious talking, daily from 6.55 a.m. to past midnight. At 9.30 on Saturday morning (except in summer) it conducts a critical survey of new recordings, 'Record Review'; Sunday morning's 'Music Weekly' at 10.15 considers topical issues, usually linked to a forthcoming broadcast. Evening con-

certs – many of them live relays from the London concert halls –
tend to begin at 7.30 p.m.

Radio 4 (92.4–94.6 on FM, 198 kHz on long wave, medium-wave
reception only in the London area) carries occasional concerts and
music documentaries. Its twice-daily arts programme, 'Kaleido-
scope' (4.30 and 9.45 p.m.) contains some music coverage, as does
the 'Meridian' programme on the BBC World Service (648 kHz on
medium wave, 198 kHz on long wave). Radio 2 (88–90.2 on FM)
broadcasts some light music and old musicals for its senior listeners. Daily details appear in the morning papers.

There is little of musical consequence to be heard on any of London's local radio stations, whether BBC or commercial. A new
classical music waveband was scheduled to open in the autumn of
1992, but the economic climate and the composition of its board do
not inspire enormous confidence in its planned output.

*Melba waxes lyrical at a 1910 gramophone session. Her reward for a week's
work was $50,000.*

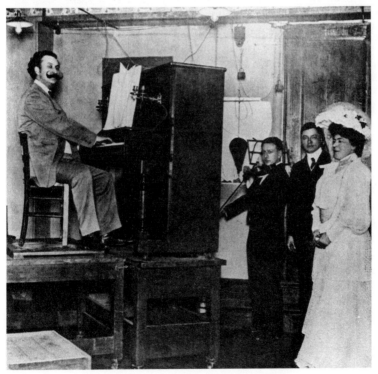

BBC 2 and Channel 4 are the television windows for music and opera, except during the Proms, when BBC 1 for once fulfils the terms of its Reithian charter. Details, again, in the daily press.

Making it
Even in this supine age of couch potatoes, amateur music continues to flourish and can be joined at almost any level. If you have a reasonable voice, can read a little music and want to broaden your social horizons and work with great conductors, contact the secretary of one of the choruses for an audition. Make your initial choice dependent on the kind of music you prefer and the conductors you would like to work with. The following is a short selection; a full listing can be found in the annual *British Music Yearbook* (£12.95).

BBC Symphony Chorus: choir master Stephen Jackson, Room 410, 16 Langham Street, W1A 1AA, tel. 071-927 4370

London Choral Society: principal conductor Jane Glover, administrator Sally Payton, 30 Bisham Gardens, N6 6DD, tel. 081-340 8986

London Philharmonic Choir: secretary Sheila Lewis, 701 Grenville House, Dolphin Square, SW1, tel. 081-798 8083

London Symphony Chorus: principal conductor Richard Hickox, secretary Margaret Daly, chairman David Leonard, 42 Arlington Avenue, N1 7AY, tel. 071-359 1242

Philharmonia Chorus: c/o Taylor Joynson Garrett, 10 Maltravers Street, WC2R 3BS, tel. 071-836 8456

Royal Choral Society: music director Laszlo Heltay, manager Michael Heyland, International House, 2/4 Wendell Road, W12 9RT, tel. 081-740 4273.

For those with solo ambitions, a number of amateur and semi-professional operatic companies advertise at the back of *Opera* magazine, monthly scrutineer of the highs and lows, which also contains listings of forthcoming events. In order to sing in any professional group, you will have to seek membership of the actors' union, Equity (tel. 071-636 6361). Proof of prior professional engagements is required.

Amateur orchestras tend to advertise for members on noticeboards of music colleges and local libraries, and at the rear of *Classical Music* magazine. Local newspapers like the *Hampstead & Highgate Express* may give an idea of what is happening in your area.

Too much playing can cause ailments known as fiddler's neck, flautist's elbow and pianist's pinkie. A Musicians' and Keyboard Clinic (7 Park Crescent, W1, tel. 071-436 5961) exists to diagnose, treat, advise and sympathize. For those with emotional difficulties arising from their art, Arts Psychology Consultants (tel. 071-244 6007) provide counselling for a range of conditions from stage fright to creative paralysis.

Getting more out of it

If you join the Friends of English National Opera (tel. 071-836 8344) or Covent Garden (tel. 071-240 1200) you will gain access to a variety of lectures, symposia, rehearsals, parties and backstage tours. Friends' groups of the various orchestras offer social, rather than intellectual, stimulus.

Adult Education Institutes in most areas give weekly evening courses in musical appreciation, theory and performance, but the range and quality of these courses are suffering from drastic cuts in local government funding. Drop by your nearest library for an Adult Education prospectus. If a course looks interesting, you have the right to attend one lesson free before enrolling. The cost tends to be around £30 a term, £10 for pensioners and the unemployed.

Finding a private teacher in order to learn an instrument is a hit-and-miss affair. Scan the noticeboard in your library and the window of your newsagent for someone nearby. The personal columns of *Classical Music* usually carry a few advertisements, and the *British Music Education Yearbook* contains comprehensive coverage of professional tuition available at all levels. It is on sale at music bookships at £11.50.

While the traditional music colleges specialize in graduate and postgraduate studies, the London College of Music (tel. 071-437 6120) offers part-time evening classes in a wide range of subjects.

If you want to make instruments, the London College of Furniture has a department of music technology that offers full-time courses across the gamut of instruments, from baroque fiddles to electronic keyboards. Apply for details to the College, 41 Commercial Road, E1 1LA, tel. 071-247 1953.

If you have no piano at home, you can book a grand by the hour near Wigmore Street, tel. 071-486 0025.

Digging for music

For serious research, the British Library (Great Russell Street, WC1, tel. 071-636 1544) remains the prime source of composers' manuscripts, letters and scarce musical books. It admits scholars only on the production of written authority from a recognized publisher or university. Once inside, you can freely search the catalogues and microfilms but have to wait anything from an hour to a week for items to be delivered. Photocopies and photographs are obtainable with further delay and the librarians' attitude is rarely friendlier than sullen. You will quickly appreciate why Karl Marx plotted violent revolution in the Reading Room.

The music room is more congenial. Its treasures include the greatest collection of Handel's manuscripts to be found anywhere in the world, most of them owned by the Queen and on permanent loan from the Royal Library. There is also a Bach *Handschrift* of the *Klavierübung* of 1731, Mozart's marriage certificate, Wagner's setting of 'Rule, Britannia!' and Alban Berg's prologue to *Lulu*.

All twelve of Haydn's London Symphonies are housed here, four entirely in his own hand, the remainder written out by his personal copyist and corrected by the composer. A similar manuscript of Beethoven's ninth symphony is on loan to the Library from the Royal Philharmonic Society.

The Central Music Library (160 Buckingham Palace Road, SW1, near Victoria Station, tel. 071-798 2192) has a substantial lending stock of books and scores, many obtained from the estates of eminent scholars. To borrow items you need to enrol at the library and be resident in London, but anyone can use the reading room.

The music colleges and music faculties at London's universities have good libraries to which visitors are readily admitted. The library at the Royal College of Music, SW7 (tel. 071-589 3643) is singularly well-stocked; it also happens somehow to possess the manuscript of Mozart's 24th piano concerto (K.491) (with rude faces doodled in the margin) and Schubert's sketches for his C-major symphony. The BBC has a vast record and music library; access depends on the co-operation of a friendly broadcaster.

The National Sound Archive (29 Exhibition Road, SW7, tel. 071-589 6603) is one of the world's oldest, largest and most hospitable disc collections, with listening facilities on the premises.

The Early Music Centre (17 Russell Square, WC1, tel. 071-580 8401) offers advice on all aspects of performance, tuition and availability of medieval, Renaissance and baroque music.

For local attainments, the British Music Information Centre (10 Stratford Place, W1, tel. 071-499 8567) is unfailingly helpful and knowledgeable, willing to answer telephone enquiries and loan scores and recordings to anyone with a serious interest.

The Musicians Benevolent Fund (16 Ogle Street, W1, tel. 071-636 4481) assists professionals in need.

8

A MUSICAL STROLL THROUGH CENTRAL LONDON

London's musical history is scattered everywhere, around the department stores of the West End, the eateries of Soho, the greenery of the great parks and the neon flashes of theatreland. A break from shopping and a few steps south take you back in time to a Handel or Berlioz première; an after-dinner stroll puts you in Wagner's footsteps. A whole day can agreeably be devoted to a gentle exploration of some of London's central musical heritage, mingled with its other delights.

Leicester Square Underground station is a good place to begin – close enough to where Mozart started his symphonic career. Heading south from the station down Charing Cross Road, you will find Cecil Court on the left-hand side. No. 19, the barber shop where Mozart lived, is now a treasure house of second-hand music and musical literature called Travis & Emery. Tear yourself away before you buy one of those textually corrupt, but visually splendid, nineteenth-century *Messiah* scores.

At the end of the passage you will reach St Martin's Lane and, to your right, the Coliseum, home of the English National Opera. Walk down towards Trafalgar Square, which commemorates the 1805 naval victory over Napoleon's fleet with a 51-metre column bearing the one-armed statue of Horatio, Lord Nelson, for whom Haydn wrote a hero's Mass and on whom the pigeons leave their daily mess. The Church of St Martin-in-the-Fields (1721), on the left, has lent its name to an international ensemble that once rehearsed there. The singing actress Nell Gwyn, Charles II's mistress, was buried in 1687 in its now defunct churchyard.

If you can spare the time, drop into the National Portrait Gallery across the road to see its images of Handel, Haydn and more recent musical eminences. Entrance is free. Then proceed west in the direction of Piccadilly, turning right up the Haymarket. Ignore the theatre bearing that name. Far more interesting is Her Majesty's Theatre on the right-hand side, arguably the most significant musical spot in the British Isles, though regrettably not connected with serious musical activity for more than half a century and bearing no trace now of its former glory.

Her Majesty's is built on the site of the 1705 Queen's (later King's) Theatre, where Handel presented twenty-four operas and his earliest oratorio, *Esther*. On his second visit Haydn gave premières of his last three symphonies here and Jenny Lind, the 'Swedish Nightingale', made her London début here in 1847. Her Majesty's staged the first British *Ring* cycle in 1882, with the Bayreuth cast under Anton Seidl. The present building was erected in 1897 and housed a number of opera seasons under Thomas Beecham until 1924, when it was turned into a commercial theatre.

Piccadilly Circus is a seedy spot for aimless youth, and undergoes constant renovation. Avoid it by turning smartly left to reach Le Meridien Hotel, the site of the former St James's Hall, which boasted a fine restaurant on its ground floor and a secret side-entrance for the orchestra and Royal Family. Ghosts of great concerts past flit about its portals. Saint-Saëns gave the world première here of his most-played symphony, the Third. At St James's church opposite, young Leopold Stokowski was organist until he emigrated to the US in 1905.

A little further along you reach Burlington House, where Handel once occupied a back room. Today it is the headquarters of the Royal Academy of Arts. Take a look at the current exhibition, and perhaps stop for a snack in the civilized refectory.

Turn up the elegant Burlington Arcade and into New Bond Street, where the music publishers Cramer and Chappell first set up shop; Chappell's still has an instrument shop at No. 50 on the right. Bartók scored his greatest British triumphs at the Aeolian Hall on the left. Further up, you will come to Brook Street. No. 25 was the house in which Handel wrote his masterpieces and where his servant found him weeping over the score of *Messiah*. He died here in 1759, surrounded by his valuable art collection. The house is virtually unchanged outside and should be preserved as a national Handel museum. Shamefully, it is not.

Reverse up Brook Street, cross New Bond Street, and you enter Hanover Square, where Handel played the organ in St George's (1724) parish church. Several celebrities married here: the poet

Shelley (1814), the politician Benjamin Disraeli (1869), Wagner's novelist friend George Eliot and the future US President, Theodore Roosevelt.

Little survives of Hanover Square's original buildings, and nothing at all of the famous concert rooms on the corner of Hanover Street where Johann Christian Bach and Carl Friedrich Abel started the world's first subscription series. Among those who conducted in its marvellous acoustics were Haydn, Mendelssohn and Wagner; its musical role ceased in 1869. The surrounding area was heavily bombed during the Second World War.

Oxford Circus is a permanent traffic-jam in a fog of motor exhaust, which clouds what remains of John Nash's architectural vista. The Argyll Rooms, where the Philharmonic Society tended Beethoven's well-being, burned down in 1830; their site is covered by an Underground entrance. Proceed up Regent Street towards the Park, without a backward glance. You will pass by Boosey & Hawkes, the music publisher and shop, before reaching the Langham Hotel, which was home to many visiting composers, including Sibelius, Elgar and Janáček.

The famous Queen's Hall, London's finest concert room, stood

across Portland Place, behind All Soul's Church (1824), from 1893 until the *Luftwaffe* bombed it to the ground in May 1941. Also crushed was a warren of restaurants and watering holes frequented by musicians, of which Pagani's was a culinary legend. The site of Queen's Hall is now occupied by a BBC suite of offices named Henry Wood House, after the founder of the Promenade concerts. His statue sits in darkness above the interior reception desk.

BBC Broadcasting House, at the junction of Regent Street and Portland Place, harbours within its entrails a couple of studios where invitation concerts are sometimes given. Enquire at the reception desk for details. Then continue heading north towards Regent's Park, crossing Queen Anne Street, were a plaque on No. 58 reveals that Berlioz lived here. Parallel to Portland Place runs Great Portland Street, where Mendelssohn lived at No. 103 and Weber died tragically at No. 91 – both houses now demolished. The George pub stands at No. 55, a shadow of its pre-war self.

Walking up either street will bring you into the earthly paradise of Regent's Park. Before spending the rest of the day boating on the lake, admiring the magnificent flower-beds, or going to the zoo, take a peek into the Royal Academy of Music to see what concerts are planned in its excellent Duke's Hall.

In the park there is afternoon entertainment by brass bands on the bandstand nearest Baker Street, the scene of an IRA bomb atrocity in 1984. Regent's Park also boasts an open-air theatre (tel. 071-486 2431), which stages Shakespeare plays on most summer evenings and some afternoons. Wagner used to wander round the lakes feeding the ducks or visiting the zoo, and Vaughan Williams wrote his last two symphonies from a room on Hanover Terrace, overlooking the green expanses.

If it looks like rain, skip the park. Meander instead down Marylebone High Street, browsing in its music shops, second-hand booksellers and comfortable tea-rooms with permanently steamed-over windows.

9

A TASTE OF THE MUSIC

Of the hundreds of pieces inspired by London and its sights, the following are quintessential (arranged below from general to more local pieces):

HAYDN's twelve London Symphonies (1791–5) do not overtly describe the city or its people, though the *Surprise* suggests the somnolent habits among sections of his audience. No. 104 was named the London Symphony and is the last he ever wrote.

VAUGHAN WILLIAMS's London Symphony (1914) contains certain distinctive sounds – the chimes of Westminster and the street-cry of 'sweet lavender' – but is not a programmatic or descriptive work. The composer preferred it to be known as 'a Symphony by a Londoner'.

John IRELAND wrote a once-popular *London Overture* (1934).

The prolific Eric COATES constructed a *London Suite* and a *London Again Suite* (1970), of which the *Knightsbridge March* was famous as a TV theme.

The jazzman Fats WALLER set down his impressions of the city in a 6-movement *London Suite* (1939).

Luciano BERIO has written *Cries of London* (1975) for chamber chorus.

William WALTON and Witold LUTOSŁAWSKI have each inscribed short pieces *In Honour of the City of London*.

Johann STRAUSS senior jotted down a London Season Waltz (1839); his son left *Memories of Covent Garden* (1867) in three-four time.

BEECHAM SUNDAY CONCERTS

Director: HAROLD HOLT

The visiting Dane Paul von KLENAU described *Bank Holiday, Souvenir of Hampstead Heath*.

Gustav HOLST celebrated in *Brook Green Suite* (1933) the district where he lived and in *St Paul's Suite* (1913) the school where he taught. He also wrote a piece on *Hammersmith* (1931).

Friedrich FLOTOW's most successful opera *Martha* (1847) is set in 'the market of Richmond', although adapted from a French pantomime about 'la Servante de Greenwich'.

Andrzej PANUFNIK composed a *Thames Pageant* (1969) for the Borough of Richmond, where he resided.

HANDEL's *Water Music* was written for a royal river party on the Thames and his *Music for the Royal Fireworks* was intended as an outdoor entertainment at Vauxhall Gardens. Both convey the restrained hedonism of their era. He also composed in 1753 an *Anthem for the Foundling Hospital*, a charitable institution that survives as the Thomas Coram Foundation. In *Handel in the Strand*, Percy GRAINGER parodied the old master strolling down a central street.

Werner EGK composed a ballet, *Casanova in London* (1969).

Noël COWARD left a *London Morning* ballet. His song 'A Nightgale Sang in Berkeley Square' struck a longer chord than George GERSHWIN's of the same place.

THE BEATLES immortalized Abbey Road (1967).

10

A GUIDE TO THE LITERATURE

* = currently available   R = *revised edition*
Place of publication is London, unless otherwise stated

*Banks, F. R., *The New Penguin Guide to London*, 10th ed., 1988. Jacket-pocket reference.

Beecham, Sir Thomas, *A Mingled Chime*, Hutchinson, 1944. Witty, un-self-revealing memoir.

Blandford, Linda, *The LSO*, Michael Joseph, 1984. Candid account of a year with the orchestra.

Blom, Eric, *Music in England*, Penguin, 1942; 2nd ed., 1947. Long out-of-print but still the standard work, elegant and erudite.

Elkin, Robert, *The Old Concert Rooms of London*, Edward Arnold, 1955. Useful history by the author of the Queen's Hall epitaph (1944).

*Fenby, Eric, *Delius as I knew him*, Faber & Faber, 1936; R. 1981. Unique encounters with the remote reprobate.

Foreman, Lewis, *From Parry to Britten; British Music in Letters, 1900–1945*, Batsford, 1987, pb. Browse through musical byways.

*Griffiths, Paul, *New sounds, new personalities: British composers of the 1980s*, Faber & Faber, 1987. Interviews with contemporary composers, from Birtwistle to Benjamin.

*Hogwood, Christopher, *Handel*, Thames and Hudson, 1985. Outstanding modern account of Handel's London legacy.

*Kennedy, Michael, *Britten*, Dent Master Musicians, 1981. Concise biography of tight-lipped subject.

—— *Portrait of Elgar*, Oxford University Press, 1936; R. 1981.

Lambert, Constant, *Music Ho!*, Faber & Faber, 1934. Timeless polemic.

*Robert Latham (ed.), *The Shorter Pepys*, Penguin, 1987. Contains musical evidence from the great seventeenth-century diarist.

Lebrecht, Norman, *Hush! Handel's in a Passion*, André Deutsch, 1985, pb. Original ancedotes of Handel and his contemporaries.

*Mitchell, Donald, and Reed, Philip, *Letters from a Life: the selected letters and diaries of Benjamin Britten*, 2 vols, Faber & Faber, 1991. Lively musical snippets of 1930s London.

Moore, Gerald, *Am I too Loud?*, Hamish Hamilton, 1962. Piano accompanist's memoirs.

*Motion, Andrew, *The Lamberts*, Chatto & Windus, 1986. Portrait of a doomed musical dynasty.

Myers, Rollo H., *Music since 1939*, Longmans, Green, 1946. Account of a transformatory epoch.

Norris, Gerald, *A musical gazetteer of Great Britain and Ireland*, David & Charles, 1981. Contains a lively district-by-district account of almost every composer who ever visited London, with addresses and activities.

Pearson, Hesketh, *Gilbert and Sullivan*, Hamish Hamilton, 1935.

*Powell, Anthony, *Casanova's Chinese Restaurant*, Heinemann, 1960. The most Proustian of English novelists recalls incisive images of musical London in the 1930s.

*Priestley, J. B., *Angel Pavement*, Heinemann, 1930. Evocative novel of London and music.

Schmitz, Oscar A. H., *The Land without Music*, trans. Hans Herzl, Jarrolds, 1925. Pungent Anglophobia.

*Shaw, George Bernard, *Music in London*, Constable, 1937. Period history and histrionics, unbeatable critical wit.

Smyth, Ethel, *Impressions that Remained*, Longmans, Green, 1919. Memoirs of the composing ice-queen.

*Tippett, Michael, *Those Twentieth-Century Blues*, Hutchinson, 1991. Typically quirkish recollection.

Wood, Sir Henry J., *My Life of Music*, Victor Gollancz, 1938. Detailed autobiography.

NOTES

Preface
1. Speech at the Guildhall, 19 January 1904.
2. James Boswell, *Life of Johnson*, 1791, p.178.

1: The Toneless Town
1. George Bernard Shaw, *Shaw's Music*, ed. Dan H. Laurence, Max Reinhardt, 1981, vol. 3, p.353.
2. Ralph Waldo Emerson, *English Traits*, 1856, quoted in Nicholas Temperley (ed.), *Music in Britain: The Romantic Age, 1800–1914*, The Athlone Press, 1981, p.11.
3. Friedrich Nietzsche, *Jenseits von Gut und Böse*, cited in Schmitz below, p.11.
4. Heinrich Heine, *Lutetia (La Lutèce)*, 1843. Heine's Anglophobia was undisguised. In the same volume he wrote of the English as being 'repulsive to me from the very depths of my soul: I do not regard them as my fellow human beings, but as mere automata.'
5. Shaw, op. cit.
6. Thomas Hobbes, *History of the Civil Wars*, p.169.
7. Oscar A. H. Schmitz (1873–1931), *Das Land ohne Musik: Englische Gesellschaftsprobleme*, Georg Müller, 1914.
8. 'Die Engländer sind das einzige Kulturvolk ohne eigene Musik (Gassenhauer ausgenommen)', ibid., p.30.
9. Ibid.
10. *The Land without Music*, trans. Hans Herzl, Jarrolds, 1925.
11. See *The Letters of Thomas Mann*, ed. and trans. Richard and Clara Winston, Alfred A. Knopf, Inc., 1970, vol. 1, pp.11–13.
12. H. H. Stuckenschmidt, *Arnold Schoenberg: his life, world and work*, trans. Humphrey Searle, John Calder, 1977, p.277.
13. *Sir Henry Wood: 50 Years of the Proms*, BBC, 1945, p.27.
14. Ibid., p.63.
15. Bernard Shore, *The Orchestra Speaks*, Longmans, Green & Co., 1938, p.189.
16. David Cox, *The Henry Wood Proms*, BBC, 1980, p.49.

17. Henry J. Wood, *My Life of Music*, Victor Gollancz, 1938, p.299.
18. Thomas Russell (ed.), *Homage to Henry Wood*, CPO Booklets, 1944, p.41.
19. Wood, op. cit., p.278.
20. Thomas Russell, *Philharmonic Decade*, Hutchinson, 1944, pp.18–19.
21. Neville Marriner, interview with the author, 1985.
22. See Cyril Ehrlich, *The Music Profession in Britain since the 18th Century*, Clarendon Press, 1985.
23. See Gerhard Hirschfeld (ed.), *Exile in Great Britain*, Berg / German Historical Institute, 1984, pp.2–3.

2: The Void between Two Elizabeths

1. In, for example, *Music of the Crusades*, Early Music Consort of London, dir. David Munrow, Decca Records, 1971.
2. Stanley Sadie (ed.), *The Concise Grove Dictionary of Music*, Macmillan, 1988, p.628.
3. Christopher Hogwood, *Music at Court*, Victor Gollancz, 1980, p.7.
4. Sir John Hawkins, *A General History of the Science and Practice of Music* (5 vols), 1776.
5. Leigh Henry, *Dr John Bull*, 1937.
6. Walter L. Woodfill, *Musicians in English Society; from Elizabeth to Charles I*, Princeton University Press, 1953, p.178.
7. Hogwood, op. cit., p.36.
8. Robert Latham (ed.), *The Shorter Pepys*, Penguin, 1987, p.480.
9. Ibid., p.864.
10. Ibid, p.848.
11. William T. Parke, *Musical Memoirs*, 1830, pp.256–7.
12. Jacob Simon (ed.), *Handel, a Celebration of his Life and Times, 1685–1759*, National Portrait Gallery, 1985, p.252.
13. John Myerscough, 'The Economic Importance of the Arts in Britain', Policy Studies Institute, July 1988.
14. Harold Atkins and Archie Newman, *Beecham Stories*, Robson Books, 1978, p.53.
15. Bayan Northcott (ed.), *The Music of Alexander Goehr*, Schott Music, 1980, p.32.
16. William H. Cummings, *Purcell*, 1881.

3: Beneath a Giant Shadow

1. Roger North, *Memoirs of Musick*, 1728, quoted in Robert Elkin, *The Old Concert Rooms of London*, Edward Arnold, 1955, p.19.
2. *London Gazette*, 26–30 December 1672.
3. Elkin, op. cit., p.25.
4. Anonymous poet, Elkin, op. cit., p.17.
5. Stanley Sadie (ed.), *New Grove Dictionary of Music and Musicians*, Macmillan, 1980, vol. 8, *Art. Handel*, p.104.
6. John Byrom, published in London newspapers on 5 June 1723.
7. Norman Lebrecht, *Hush! Handel's in a Passion*, André Deutsch, 1985, p.64.

8. William S. Rockstro, *The Life of George Frederick Handel*, Macmillan, 1883, p.390.
9. Charles Burney, *An Account of the Performances in Westminster Abbey and the Pantheon*, in *Commemoration of Handel*, 1785, p.36.
10. Ibid., p.34.
11. Ibid., p.34..
12. Rockstro, op. cit., p.397.
13. Henry Edward Krehbiel, *Music and Manners in the Classical Period*, Archibald Constable, 1898, p.83.
14. Oscar Sonneck (ed.), *Beethoven, Impressions by his Contemporaries*, Dover Publications Inc., 1926, p.152.
15. Attrib. – to which Vincent Novello added, 'One can only regret that he had not the candour to own from whom he borrowed the pebble.' Introduction to *Purcell's Sacred Music*, quoted in Rockstro, op. cit., p.418.
16. Lebrecht, op. cit., p.71.
17. Letter of 10 April 1782, cited in Philidor biography in *British Chess Magazine*, 1960–1, p.77.
18. Ibid., p.154.
19. *The Reminiscences of Harry Angelo*, 1828–30.
20. See Grainger's reminscence in Evan Charteris, *John Sargent*, William Heinemann, 1927, pp.149–51.
21. A. C. Dies, *Biographische Nachrichten von Joseph Haydn*, Vienna, 1810.
22. Letter to Maria Ann von Genzinger, in H. C. Robbins Landon, *Haydn, a documentary study*, Thames and Hudson, 1981, p.118.
23. Percy Scholes, *The Great Dr Burney*, Oxford University Press, 1948, vol. II, p.110.
24. *Morning Chronicle*, 12 March 1791, see Robbins Landon, op. cit., p.123.
25. Krehbiel, op. cit., p.93.
26. Elkin, op. cit., p.97.
27. Christopher Hogwood, *Handel*, Thames and Hudson, 1985, p.243.
28. H. B. and C. L. E. Cox (eds), *Leaves from the Journals of Sir George Smart*, Longmans Green & Co., 1907. Entry for 16 September 1825.
29. Resolution of the Philharmonic Society, 28 February 1827.
30. Letter to Ignaz Moscheles, 18 March 1827. See Emily Anderson, *The Letters of Beethoven*, Macmillan, 1961.
31. Both quotations from Gerald Norris, *Stanford, the Cambridge Jubilee and Tchaikovsky*, David & Charles, 1980, p.97.
32. Ibid., p.101.
33. Julius Benedict, *Weber*, Sampson, Low, Marston & Co., n.d., p.133.
34. Rudolph Sabor, *The Real Wagner*, André Deutsch, 1987, p.211.
35. Wagner, *Mein Leben*, Munich, 1911, pp.175–80.
36. *Cosima Wagner's Diaries* (ed. Gregor-Dellin and Mack, trans. Skelton), Collins, 1978, vol.1, p.130.
37. See Mendelssohn's *Letters from Italy and Switzerland* (trans. Lady Wallace); Longman, Green, Reader and Dyer, 1867, 4th edition, p.313; and Mendelssohn's *Letters, 1833 to 1847* (trans. Lady Wallace), Longman, Green, Longman, Roberts & Green, 1864, 2nd edition, p.401.

38. *Cosima Wagner's Diaries* (ed. Gregor-Dellin and Mack, trans. Skelton), Collins, 1980, vol. 2, p.680.
39. Reginald Nettel, *The Orchestra in England*, Jonathan Cape, 1948, p.186.
40. Shaw review in *The Star*, 11 May 1892.
41. Ibid., 9 November 1892.
42. Interview with the author.

4: Requiem for Hallowed Halls

1. John Pudney, *Music on the South Bank*, Max Parrish Ltd / London County Council, 1951, p.44.
2. 'The Design of the Hall', *The Times*, 2 May 1951.
3. See Norman Lebrecht, 'The Retuning of a Concert Hall', *The Sunday Times*, 17 April 1983.
4. Helen Henschel, *When Soft Voices Die*, John Westhouse, 1944, p.81.
5. Anthony Powell, *Casanova's Chinese Restaurant*, William Heinemann, 1960.
6. Ivor Newton, *At the Piano*, Hamish Hamilton, 1966, p.5.
7. C. E. M. Joad, 'Queen's Hall was my Club', in *Sir Henry Wood: 50 years of the Proms*, BBC, 1944, p.53.
8. J. B. Priestley, *Angel Pavement*, William Heinemann, 1930.
9. Charles Reid, *Thomas Beecham, an independent biography*, Victor Gollancz, 1962, p.46.
10. Gerald Moore, *Am I too Loud?*, Penguin, 1966, p.100.
11. Robert Hewison, *Under Siege; Literary Life in London, 1939–45*, Weidenfeld & Nicolson, 1977, p.28.
12. Berta Geissmar, *The Baton and the Jackboot*, Hamish Hamilton, 1944, pp.376–7, 389–90.
13. See Dettmar Dressel, *Up the Down Scale*, Selwyn & Blount, 1937, pp.232–3.
14. Meirion Bowen, 'Two concerts', *Guardian*, 8 April 1988.

5: An Exotick and Irrational Entertainment

1. John Amis and Michael Rose, *Words about Music*, Faber & Faber, 1989, p.279.
2. *The Spectator*, 6 March 1711.
3. Letter dated 23 January 1752.
4. Interview in *Time* magazine, 1961.
5. Lewis Foreman, *From Parry to Britten*, Batsford, 1987.
6. Herman Klein, *Thirty Years of Musical Life in London*, Heinemann, 1903, pp.48–9.
7. C. V. Stanford, *Studies and memories*, Constable & Co., 1908, pp.21–2.
8. Ibid., pp.21–2.
9. Frances Donaldson, *The Royal Opera House in the 20th Century*, Weidenfeld & Nicolson, 1988, p.9.
10. Foreman, op. cit., pp.38–9.
11. *Observer* interview, 20 March 1910.

12. Foreman, op. cit., pp.105–6.
13. Eugene Goossens, *Overtures and Beginners*, Methuen, 1951, p.250.
14. Foreman, op. cit., p.136.
15. Michael Kennedy, *Britten*, Dent, 1981, p.44.
16. Benjamin Britten, in *Sadler's Wells Opera Book No. 3*, 1945, p.8.
17. E. W. White, *Benjamin Britten, his life and operas*, Faber & Faber, 1970, p.42.
18. Kennedy, op. cit., p.47.
19. Reminescence by Peter Pears, BBC Radio 3, 7 August 1974, in Christopher Palmer (ed.), *The Britten Companion*, Faber & Faber, 1984, p.104.
20. Kennedy, op, cit., p.46.
21. Christopher Hogwood, *Handel*, Thames and Hudson, 1985, p.87.
22. J. Ridgway, *Memoirs of Mrs Billington from her birth*, 1792.
23. Charles Neilson Gattey, *Queens of Song*, Barrie & Jenkins, 1979, p.84.
24. H. S. Holland and W. S. Rockstro, *Jenny Lind the Artist*, John Murray, 1893, p.271.
25. Gattey, op. cit., p.109.
26. Klein, op. cit., p.314.
27. John Hetherington, *Melba*, Faber & Faber, 1967, p.177..
28. Beecham, *A Mingled Chime*, Hutchinson, 1944.
29. Rupert Christiansen, *Prima Donna: a history*, Penguin, 1986, p.318.
30. Noël Coward, *Design for Living*, 1933.

PICTURE CREDITS

INDEX

INDEX

INDEX